T0192991

Antonia
and her
Daughters

Marlena de Blasi is the bestselling author of *A Thousand Days in Venice, Tuscan Secrets, An Umbrian Love Story, That Summer in Sicily* and a novel *Amandine*. She has been a chef, a journalist, a food and wine consultant and a restaurant critic. She is also the author of two internationally published cookbooks of Italian food. She and her husband, Fernando, moved from Venice to San Casciano where *Tuscan Secrets* was written and now live in Orvieto.

Antonia and her Daughters developed as Marlena became friends with and a trusted confidant of the real Antonia who wanted Marlena to tell her story. Although Marlena was working on quite a different book, Antonia's story began insisting that this was the right time and should be the basis of Marlena's next book.

Also by Marlena de Blasi

Non-fiction

A Thousand Days in Venice

Tuscan Secrets

(previously published as *Dolce e Salata*)

An Umbrian Love Story

That Summer in Sicily

A Taste of Southern Italy

(originally published as *Regional Foods of Southern Italy*)

Regional Foods of Northern Italy

Fiction

Amandine

MARLENA de BLASI

Antonia and her Daughters

ALLEN&UNWIN
SYDNEY•MELBOURNE•AUCKLAND•LONDON

This edition published in 2013
First published in Australia and New Zealand by Allen & Unwin in 2012

Allen & Unwin
Sydney, Melbourne, Auckland, London

83 Alexander Street
Crows Nest NSW 2065
Australia
Phone: (61 2) 8425 0100
Email: info@allenandunwin.com
Web: www.allenandunwin.com

Cataloguing-in-Publication details are available
from the National Library of Australia
www.trove.nla.gov.au

ISBN 978 1 74331 738 9

Cover design by Lisa White
Internal design by Natalie Winter
Cover photographs: iStockphoto.com
Set in 11/16.7 pt Minion Pro by Bookhouse, Sydney

10 9 8 7 6 5 4 3 2

For Larry G. Martin of Deer Park, Illinois

As was Barlozzo, he must surely be one of the Thirty-Six.
He stopped by one evening and changed things forever.

Author's note

Antonia and her Daughters is a true story. To protect the sacred right to privacy of this family and their way of life, I have changed names and placed the narrative at a geographic distance from the actual location in Tuscany where these events in fact unfolded.

In 2010, at the age of eighty-nine, Antonia passed away peacefully in the predawn hours of a May morning, twelve days after our last meeting. The story she had recounted to me during the summer of 2003 she now passed on to her daughters in a series of letters which she began writing in 2004 and all of which were found among her private papers.

Though Antonia often told me herself of her wish that I write this book—*'after I'm gone'*—she also mentioned this desire in the legacy of her letters. Her daughters, granddaughters and great-granddaughter were in accord with this desire, and all of these women, most especially the characters I've named Filippa and Luce, urged me on with unfailing grace.

There is much in the narrative which was difficult for me to include. At many junctures I was tempted to commit my own sins of omission or, at the least, to sprinkle a touch of rosewater here and there. Several passages I was moved to delete from my early notes and yet—and not without angst—I retrieved them. That's what a storyteller is morally bound to do when she agrees to take on the task of telling someone else's truths.

PROLOGUE

Winter

A leaving sun tries for a last glisten through dull yellow snow clouds. In front of the dilapidated doors at number 34 in the via del Duomo, we wave *addio* to the big blue truck, a tangle of straps and canvas tarps rattling against its emptiness as it lumbers up the gentle slope of the stones towards the cathedral. As though waiting for a cue, we stay there, Fernando and I, arms about each other's waist, long after the truck is out of sight.

Oh yes, I think, this must be the moment when we turn around, push open the doors, climb the stairs to the ballroom. The restored, scrubbed, polished, upholstered, already-woodsmoke-scented-from-this-morning's-first-fire ballroom. For two years this was the moment we'd chanted for, dreamed of, counted out the last of our doubloons to fund. And now? For the first time, there's no one up there hammering and cursing and singing. No one. Not the five Neapolitan workmen who'd become as errant sons to us nor the upholsterers who—like pastry cooks porting a flaming pudding through a hall—had carried drapes and valances, piece by piece, and chairs and sofas, one by one, through the winding back alleys from their atelier here to number 34, past neighbours gathered along the route for a glimpse of their day's work. So much red, almost everything is some shade of red, they'd clucked, mystified. Also gone away is the woodworker who made two legs of the kitchen table shorter than the other two and swore he meant to, saying the slant gave the room the correct perspective. I dared to ask him about the plates which would surely slide down to and collide with the ones set before the person at the foot of the decline. As he puttered about filling soup plates and glasses with varying amounts of water and demonstrating the nuances of physics, he'd said, with the disdain appropriate when addressing a cultural outlander—a stance which commonly greets the expatriate and one he must quickly learn to greet with a certain meekness—'Here one arranges life to fit art.' Also gone is the marble worker with the thick-lashed eyes of a pony, who tramped repeatedly about, room to room, with his fistful of chains and an executioner's grunt to distress the surfaces of the stone, and the electrician who, having had so little to do—what with the chandeliers and sconces being stuck with candles—took to helping the plumber. Everyone gone. We'd been an extended, exuberant and highly functional family but there's no one left now—only us. Our belongings unpacked, the kitchen upright, white beans and pancetta and branch of sage braising in red wine in a terracotta pot on the back burner, the yellow wooden *baldacchino* we've carried from Venice to Tuscany to here mounted, its red silk feather bed plumped, firewood stacked on the back terrace, linens in the chest, brocade and damask stretched over, nailed to and draped upon every remotely submissive surface. When we climb those stairs we will finally be *at home*. So why are Fernando and I standing here in the cold?

'Shouldn't we be going up now?' he asks.

I look at Fernando, who has been looking at me. Waiting for my reverie to pass. 'Of course. Let's have a bath, a rest and . . .'

'And then let's walk up to the piazza and sit in Foresi for a bit. *Va bene?*'

'Do you think any of the old troupe will come by? Miranda, perhaps. Or Neddo. Maybe Barlozzo? Do you think anyone will?'

'After staying so close through these two years of waiting and working I would think they'll trust us to our own mode of celebration on the first night in the ballroom.'

'They'll be right, won't they?'

'Of course they will. Come with me now.'

The bulbous toes of my workboots hit the wall of each shallow step. I count them as I climb: *uno, due, tre, quattro*, as though I don't know there are twenty-eight. I reach the threshold of our double door, still flung wide, a breeze shivering the moor's-head knockers against their rusted plates. Snow falls from the open skylight. Sugar shaken from a sieve. I look over the balustrade to the courtyard below to see that the grocer next door has cornered Fernando for a football chat. Not wanting to go inside—not yet, not without him—I sit sideways on the top step, my back caressed by the roughness of the old wall. A leg crossed over a knee, I close my eyes, pull in a long breath to soothe the thudding of my heart, tell myself that nothing much will change now that we are at home. We'll carry on with our explorations of the town and the outlying *comuni*, wander the markets in the mornings, take our *espressi* and pastries at Montanucci. We'll cook and bake. Balancing our town life with one in the countryside, we'll ramble through the woods and the fields and among the vines in every season. Swishing through wet grasses on autumn mornings, sending small birds fluttering up onto high branches, we'll poke sticks beneath the gnarled veins of oak roots and mouldering leaves where the fat porcini crouch, smelling of loam and something dark and forbidden. Even as we fill our basket we'll be tasting them, laid on a grate and roasted over a fire, their hollows stuffed with smears of garlic and fine green oil, their juices dripping onto thick trenchers of bread in the pan underneath. We'll pick blackberries in the ditches, pierce our hands on the thorns of rose hips, gather chestnuts big as plums, carve crosses on their hearts and cook them till their skins char and burst. In April we'll thrust the ancient hand-wrought trowel which Neddo gave us into the soft spring earth and down to the roots of the new grasses. We'll tie them in bundles with the lengths of kitchen string which Miranda has taught me to carry in my skirt pocket. Salad for supper.

We shall rent a plot from those farmers in Canonica, and twine tomato plants up onto bamboo stakes and coddle burgeoning melons under glass bells and plant twenty rows of squash flowers. And when the yellow blossoms are big as lilies, we'll pluck them, douse them with water from the spring at Tione, shake them dry, build a wood fire in the pit at the edge of the meadow, drag them through beer batter and fry them right there. Crisp, gold, pan-to-hand-to-mouth, as many as we can eat. New bread, new lettuces, oil from my flask, flakes of sea salt rubbed between our palms. Nothing else but wine. It will be cool, maybe cold up there as the light goes and a red moon hoists itself up into the May night. The yellow lanterns along the road to the Roman gate below will look like scattered stars and Luca and Orfeo will be there, Miranda and Neddo and Tilde. Barlozzo. These will still be our ordinary days. And the days will last as long as we do. For as long as the collision between destiny and our own follies will allow. Inevitable follies. All in all, a lovely prospect for a last chapter or two of a life. Both for those parts of life which the Pollyanna in me shall always romanticise and for those parts which are real as dirt and sky. Yes, a lovely prospect. *And so what is it, this rasping in my chest?*

A kind of fear, is it? Unnamed, unformed, faceless? What's that Welsh word? *Hiraeth*. Not fear so much as *longing*, I think. A kind of grieving. Is it that I'll miss the shambles, the imbroglio, the anticipation, the boxcar life of making do, the characters racing in and out, extras in a farce? Yes. Did I lose myself in the turbulence of all that motion? Yes again. Do I want to stay longer cosseted in that fanciful place where we were at home but not at home, that detached, vaporous region somewhere between a beginning and an end? Transition. *Lavori in corso*: work in progress. I think I do. And yet beginnings are your forte, have you forgotten that? The woman with the fairytale life, have you forgotten that as well?

He sees her from across the room and knows she's the one . . . isn't that Everywoman's fantasy? And then, in a tiny medieval church, its red-brick face turned to the Venetian lagoon, in the opal twilight of the flames of a hundred candles and musky plumes of frankincense, I married him and lived for a thousand days in Venice with him. Nine years of pages have fluttered by now, and tonight here we are setting up in the just-renovated ballroom of a sixteenth-century palazzo in a hilltown in Umbria . . . yes, a fairytale life. Complete with its rightful share of demons and frights and stumbles in the dark. Everywoman's fantasy is Everywoman's real life. How much alike we are, all of us. Opal twilight and eyes across a room notwithstanding.

Like everyone else, I've a right to my wondering, haven't I? To the fear with no name, to a thudding heart. Even to some belated seven-year itch between Fernando and me. Is there trouble in Camelot, some tremor below the common ground? Even the most pure of loves is fickle. Marked with a cleft stick. Another human condition. One which we fight and deny and rarely own. As though it were a sin to waver, to be unsure, to become tired, to close the door. To lock it. But no, that's not it. You know that's not it. Whatever it is, this unnamed fear, it's between me and myself. Me and the Fates. Jesumaria, what's happening to me?

How long ago was it that I began to understand that neither will nor deeds nor merits nor sins shape our lives? Was it when I asked Sister Mary Paul why, even though it was the other one who was the cheater, it was me who'd been punished?

'It's destiny's way,' she'd said, pulling her handkerchief from its eternal and secreted place in one of her sleeves, blowing her nose, making that noise like a ship leaving port, then replacing the handkerchief. *Destiny, child.*

'Is destiny the same as God?' I asked.

'I think God is another name for destiny. One of its names. Destiny is a name older than God.'

'So why don't we pray to destiny?'

'Because God is a better listener.'

We'd been standing in the little cell that was her office, that smelled of floor wax and ink and of the branches heavy with green apples spilling in through her open window. Now she sat in the chair in front of her desk rather than the big one behind it and pulled me down to sit on her knees. I could better see her short brownish whiskers that stuck out straight like a cat's and up close she looked more sad than she did from further away.

'So is destiny a saint?' I asked.

'No, not a saint.'

'Is he like a devil?'

'Not like a devil, not at all like a devil, although sometimes . . .'

'Sometimes what?' I tried hard not to look at her whiskers but I did anyway.

'Destiny, it's not so easy to explain,' she said.

'Like the miracles and the mysteries and that stuff in the Bible?'

'Something like that *stuff*.'

'I know. It's faith again. Just *believe* and don't ask so many "whys"?'

'I'm afraid so.'

'But it bothers me. Not so much about this morning but about Jesus. I understand the part when he was a baby and when la Madonna made him a cradle in the straw and sang to him and all those animals came to lie down near him. And when he grew up he was so kind and good and still those soldiers killed him and made la Madonna cry and why didn't God help Jesus? God can do anything, can't he, so why—?'

'That's another "why", isn't it?'

'Is it the same as why God didn't help me this morning?'

'I don't believe it was. This morning, it was . . .'

'*Destiny?* So destiny is stronger than God?'

'I don't know, child. I think they may be the same. I don't think we're supposed to know.'

I don't remember what else we talked about, but for years—and sometimes still—I wish I had touched her hand that day. Her cheek. Even then I knew I would be fine but I wondered if she would be, or ever was.

So at six, sitting on Sister Mary Paul's knees, I'd been introduced to destiny. The stones are already thrown, are they? *Hang on and let life shape itself.* Still there are those small spaces which the Fates assign to us. Those tiny runnels in between. *Do a good job. Do enough. Then do more.*

So is it enough? All this sauntering over the old cobbles from *caffè* to bar, dear little shop to the next dear little shop . . . tramping over the river and through the woods, playing at foraging, the chic peasant in a water-green taffeta skirt and Barlozzo's old cardigan? My *fornarina*'s hands pushing through his cut-off gloves. Is it enough? I don't know how to *measure* these things that make me me, myself. If I could look at myself in a mirror less merciful than my own, who would I see? A woman different from the me I know? From the one who's grown somewhat amusing with age, costumed for a role in *La Bohème* on her way to market, setting her supper table in a wheatfield, listening for a nightingale, hands in the flour, thoughts in the clouds, timing everything in a day, in an evening so as not to miss the shifting light. *Hurry. The light won't wait, you know.*

I walk back to the balustrade, lean over it to look for Fernando. Lighting each other's cigarettes, he and his friend are deep in discourse. I watch wet snow pinging against the stones, the plucking of a minor-key harp string. I wonder who they were, the women who looked over this balustrade before me. Waiting in delight, terror, chagrin. The one who climbed the twenty-eight steps in a Renaissance gown, its hem trailing mud. The one in the little black dress and a sable shrug, a hat with a veil. Nubile, plain, doddering, radiant, smoothing skirts, pinching cheeks, tearing hair; I wonder. And how did it get to be my turn to stand here reaching out to hold hands with their ghosts in this broken-down place so quiet save the harp string and the muffle of my consort's voice? The beast still thrashing in my chest.

The Fates. *Smoothing skirts, pinching cheeks, tearing hair,* what doses of delight and terror and chagrin have they measured out for me?

Fernando climbs the first flight of stairs and from the landing tells me, 'Giovanni needs some wine and things carried over from the *magazzino*. He's not feeling so well. You go on in and I'll be up in a few minutes.'

I watch him from the balustrade, tell him not to rush. Halfway through the *portone*, he turns. 'By the way, Giovanni said that Neddo passed by, asked him to tell us he'll be back about seven. A cousin or someone was with him. Giovanni didn't know exactly who.'

A bottle of red bulging in each of his down-jacket pockets, Neddo pulls a paper sack from an inside pocket, heaves its contents across the threshold. '*Sale*. Salt. To keep the ghosts away.'

'I've already hung lavender at every door to welcome them.'

Both of us in his embrace. '*Tanti auguri*,' he says again and again. 'Many good wishes.

'Ah, *lui si chiama* Biagio.' He ushers in his companion. 'Chou, Fernando, I present my Tuscan kin. My sister Giorgia's husband.'

Diminutive, bronze as August wheat, this Biagio, too, has pockets stuffed with bottles and I laugh for having wondered how we would spend this first evening officially at home at 34.

Neddo has spoken with Miranda who had spoken with Tilde. No, he hasn't heard from Barlozzo but he thinks it was his truck he saw parked by the *scuola materna* as he and Biagio walked by. I begin calculating. There's beans. Bread. Half a *finocchiona*, Tuscan salame perfumed with wild fennel. Baked pears. We'll be fine.

The buzzer. Barlozzo carries his wine offering in a plastic sack slung over a shoulder, as though a foundling sleeps in it. Miranda lays a wooden fruit box gently onto my outstretched arms. '*Piano. Piano,*' she warns.

A soup of chestnuts and porcini in a bowl covered with a dish and tied up in a kitchen towel. Roast rabbit stuffed with sausage.

Neddo defers to his brother-in-law, as does Barlozzo, and thus Biagio holds court around the table, then the fire. Like his father and grandfather before him, he is the *fattore*, overseer, on a large estate in western Tuscany—Il Castelletto. An easy raconteur, his repertoire of stories—no matter where they begin or end—all seem to centre about a woman. The same woman. A woman called Antonia.

'Her parents were farmers on a small holding in the Lunigianan hills. Tall, sinuous, wild dark hair, when she was seventeen—I was only nine at the time but I remember her as she was then—Antonia was courted by and married to *signor* Tancredi, younger son of my patrons, the de Gaspari. A farmer's daughter wedding the son of the local nobility. Every tongue in six valleys clucked about nothing else for days. No, no, that's not true—not all of the truth anyhow. You see, the clucking didn't end after days. Nor years even. The whole truth is that in all the time between then and now, with the wars and pests and birthing and dying and loving and betraying that came to pass, people are still talking about Antonia. She's a *personaggio*, the kind people need as a hero, an anti-hero. Wilful, eccentric, beautiful. Still beautiful. Patron saint, siren, rebel, zealot—the emphasis shifts according to the moment. In any case, she's all Tuscan. As are her daughters; she has two: Filippa and Luce. And they have daughters: Filippa's are called Viola and Isotta, Luce's girl is Sabina. Isotta has a daughter, too. Magdalena. Seven women. Four generations. All of them blue-eyed amazons and all of them living together in that grand villa with . . . you'll see for yourself one day. I hope you will.'

Our sweet friends gone on their way, Fernando is on the terrace smoking a last cigarette for the evening and I'm pouring out a goodnight cognac into our two tiny silver cups. I lie down on the warm tiles facing the fire to wait for him. I wonder about this Antonia. What did little Biagio call her? A saint, a zealot? A siren. He said she's beautiful. I wonder what doses of *delight and terror and chagrin* the Fates have measured out to her. Not likely she'd suffer a beast thrashing in her chest. Or would she?

Birthdates

Antonia: 1920

ANTONIA'S DAUGHTERS
Filippa: 1939
Luce: 1945

FILIPPA'S DAUGHTERS
Viola: 1962
Isotta: 1964

LUCE'S DAUGHTER
Sabina: 1966

ISOTTA'S DAUGHTER
Magdalena: 1984

CHAPTER I

Spring

I am on deadline for a manuscript. Besmirching a pact sworn, me to myself, about how I would conduct my writing life, I am fiddling with my own boundaries. Allowing distractions. Perhaps inviting them. These take two forms: the first is Emily, my dearest, oldest friend from America, who came to stay a week nearly two months ago; the second is a three-man squad at work on the daily labour of repairing what has turned out to be a less than masterful restoration of the six-metre-high vault in our *salone*.

At first light Emily creaks up the stairs from her room to ours, brushes her long red nails across the wooden door. I open it to her sheepish grin and am reminded of my daughter when she was four and five and maybe six, when she would enter my room across the three-foot corridor from hers in the deepest night. *Mom, I thought you might be lonely.*

Emily stands in the doorway, my boots in her hands. 'Will you walk with me?'

It's mostly she who talks. 'I like myself better in Italy. I forget what he's done. I forget to care. I forget to care why he did it and what he thinks. What he thinks of me. Of her. Of anything. Here it's like, out of the box and into the light. Oh, I'll go back to him eventually. Not that I can forgive him, but I *will* go back. I'd never have the courage to, you know, to, to . . . to do what you did. I mean, what if it didn't work out? What would I do?'

'If what didn't work out?'

'If starting over *without* him didn't work out.'

'But life *with* him isn't working out. You've already discovered that. And yet you'll go back. What will you do? Pretend? Mount some clever vendetta against him? *Cry me a river. I cried a river over you.*'

'That would be nice.'

'You know it wouldn't.'

'No. No, not so nice, I suppose. What I really want is to meet someone else. I'd like my own Fernando. Someone to sweep me away, to *court* me, to make me feel fresh and young, desirable.'

'Is that the whole of what you believe happened to me?' I ask her. I place my hands on her shoulders, shake her. 'Look at me, Emmy. All those things were and are true. But they compose only a *part* of the story. And maybe not even the best part of the story. In fact, not at all the best part of—'

'I know, I know, you've told me that already and I understand it, but still, you make it look so *easy*. You and Fernando seem so *perfect* together, I mean the way he looks at you, always touching you, you smiling up at him as though you'd been married an hour ago . . . and then you write and cook and you, you *live in a ballroom*. You've made it so beautiful and warm and everyone loves to be here . . . and . . .'

'Emmy, Emmy, stop it. Stop measuring and comparing. Stop coveting. One thing at a time. If you return to that life, all that sent you scurrying here will be waiting for you. There'll be work to do. And I don't mean just for him. But knowing you as I do and knowing him as I do, I think the best you'll achieve is a kind of détente. Will that be enough for you? A *pleasant* life. And should you both convince yourselves it would suffice, it will all be blown to hell with the first bold gust. And there are always bold gusts, Em, don't forget that. Reconciliation is overrated. By the time the tears dry and the promises are sworn, what caused the rupture is already pulling at the seams again. It's a quixotic dream, the one about resuming a life that once was painful but then becomes less so.'

We sit on the top step of the *duomo*, alone in the piazza save for the street cleaner who swings an old straw witch's broom over the stones, and the widow Pasqualetti, wrapped in shawls and trotting at some speed on her way home from feeding the cats down on the *cava*. Two ghosts, black against the reddening sky.

'So I'll try a different dream, the one where I come to live in Italy. After all, *living* here, just going out to buy a sack of tomatoes becomes a foray into another world . . . and then I'd find the right man and—'

'And in no time you'll have learned the Italian wife's lament: *sono tutti egocentrici, grandi mammoni*—they're all egocentrics, all attached to their mothers. Won't you be expecting too much of geography? And of the *next man*. Not to speak of the poor sack of tomatoes . . . Better, I think, to begin at home. *At home* signifying you, yourself. Better to begin with yourself. To step up to the bat, naked, if you will. Do your own work first, Em.'

'I don't know if I want to. Besides, don't you always say *No one changes; we're all eternally ourselves?*'

'I do. But we can grow, we can work at plumping up our merits, try to reassign defects to a lesser position. But *character* is intrinsic. Fixed like the colour of our eyes.'

'A fearsome thought. *We are who we are.* Like Popeye. *I am what I am, I'm a sailor man.* Jesus, is that what you truly believe? We can't go back. We can't change. What's left?'

'In your case it seems you've two choices: to accept— him and yourself just as you are—and bite the bullet; to not accept and get to work.'

'And you? Have you "done your work"?'

'I was more fortunate than you. I began when I was young. I was very old when I was young. I learned to trust myself, to make friends with destiny. To ask more of myself than anyone else. And I've always felt *rich*, somehow. Even when I didn't have a dime. Mostly then.

Sometimes I would feel almost embarrassed about all I had. All that I felt *inside*. I suppose that's why I began to write. Anyway, I'm younger now. To answer your question, yes, I've done my work. I'm still at it.'

Emily shakes her head, says, 'I'm too tired to put myself through all that introspection. I can't imagine I'd like much of what I'd find. I'd rather just plunk along and see what happens.'

She turns her back to lean against me. We stay quiet, the scraping of the broom like a metronome. She shifts to look at me then. Her voice thin as an old silver spoon, she raises a phantom glass, her face broken by a sob. 'Eat, drink and remarry.'

In the evenings when the fire is low, Emily says, like a child to a mother, *Don't leave me*, and so I don't. She needs the solace of the table, of good red wine and bread still warm from the oven. For the first weeks of her visit she'd barely left her bed save to eat and drink, and even now she wanders snuffling into the kitchen, lifts pot lids, opens oven doors, fondles wine bottles set out to warm for lunch, pushes out a half-choked *thank you* as though I'd gifted her a pulsing kidney. Can I do less than cook for her? And while I am doing so for her, why not the trio of plasterers? While washing up from these daily festivals I grind my teeth, recalling so many books I've read with front or back pages entitled *acknowledgements*, treacly thanks to this or that foundation *for the two years of blissful serenity in which I wrote this book.* Others name a herd of sixty-one researchers, readers, middle-of-the-night affirmers of faith, general cheerers-on *during the eight years and endless drafts of this book.* As usual, my publisher has granted me a year from contract to completion. I work alone in a tiny red room over a supermarket and a restaurant where the daily norm includes the arrival of forty revolving Americans under the care of a certain local tour guide who come to lunch, to drink prodigious quantities of less than honourable wine and, finally, to huddle, guffawing, under my window until said tour guide—reinvigorated, if late, after a bowl of *pastasciutta* with his mother and a brief *appuntamento galante* with his lover—arrives to fetch the forty back to the autobus.

I have never had a reader or a number I could call for affirmation in the middle of the night. It is my own fault that I have assigned the status of *jobette* to my work—an hour now and then as succour between crises. *Basta*. I need a few months alone in a garret in the seventh. A garret without a stove. Or in a cabin on a seacliff without a stove. A hollow chestnut tree. Almost any place at all without a stove. Unconvinced of the likelihood that one of these will present itself, I consider alternatives, but there are none. And then I think of Neddo. I could set up at his place in Canonica. A long-time widower with grown sons, his old farmhouse has more rooms abandoned than lived in. A superlative cook, jealous of his kitchen and his methods, Neddo will be my saviour.

'Of course you can, *amore mio*,' he answers, though I have yet to put forth much more than sketches of the plan.

'It would only be for a few months. Five, maybe six days a week. From about six in the morning until the late afternoon. I wouldn't be working straight through, of course. Maybe we could walk together for an hour or so, or I could rest by the fire if you're—'

'Yes, yes, yes. Yes to everything. Start today. Biagio's here, by the way, arrived last night, brought some birds to hang and two *kili* of Garfagnano cornmeal. Wine, too, some of that fancy de Gaspari red, and he was just asking me whether Fernando would come to play cards this afternoon. *Dio buono*, when he hears the news about you, he might never leave. Imagine the lunches and . . .'

'*Fantastico*, Neddo,' I lie through my teeth. '*Glorioso*. Biagino. Card games. Garfagnano cornmeal and putrid birds. It will be perfect.'

Once Neddo tells him of my call, little Biagio has another idea. It is he who comes to visit later that same day and announces that what I need more than a room at Neddo's is the greater tranquillity of his place. Not the place where he lives with his wife at Castelletto but a one-room stone sanctum in a nearby pine wood where he stays when he hunts.

'A four-metre hearth and two cords of aged oak, a bed, a chair, a table. Pots and pans. A demijohn of red, one of oil. Less than four kilometres to the village. I go down at seven to take the bread for Antonia and I'll take it for you, too. *Due alimentari, un forno, un macellaio, un norcino, un bar, due trattorie, un antiquario, una parrucchiera*—two groceries, a bakery, a butcher, a pork butcher, a bar, two *trattorie*, an antiques seller, a hairdresser. And there's a small market on Tuesdays and Saturdays. *Porchetta, formaggi, verdure*: wood-roasted pig, cheeses, vegetables. You'll be fine. We'll award Fernando visiting rights on weekends.'

'What-do-you-think? It-would-be-just-until-I-can-finish-the-manuscript-two-months-maybe-three-I-would-get-so-much-done-no-noise-no-Emily-no-stove . . .'

I am trying to get the story out before he begins to pull it apart, begins to make me feel selfish, foolish. A prima donna. Always more honed are his devices. *You say a real cook can cook in a tin can, so what about a writer? If you're a writer you can write anywhere, under any circumstances. Wouldn't that be true? If you* were *a writer.*

We are alone on the terrace at Foresi and, though it's not quite eight, one of the sons makes polite moves towards closing. Even so, Fernando lights a fresh cigarette, inhales through his nose, his usual preamble to offence. The match's flame still burning he says, 'Emily is leaving on the weekend. I spoke with her this morning. She is ready to, to *resume* her life. I said very little.' He blows out the match.

'You had no right to say anything.'

'I believe I did. And she does as well. She thanked me.'

I want to shake him. 'Emily's going away doesn't solve my problem . . .'

'Your problem is that you are adept at creating excuses for not writing. It's been the case since we moved into 34. And for longer than that.'

Now I want to turn over the table, smash the cigarette against his slightly too large aquiline nose. I wonder if he's right. So what if he's right.

'I won't operate any longer as though writing were an amusement, some sort of dilettantish way to fill the time while the bread is rising or the spaces between *espressi* and *passeggiate*. It's my work. No, that's wrong. It's a kind of hunger. A greediness. I can't *not* write. And beyond that, it's what we have, *all* we have to keep us.' We have walked the few metres back to 34 and are climbing the stairs. 'Rethink your precocious and empty-handed retirement, why don't you? Why not consider knocking on the door of some bank with your twenty-six years of history. I think a man—a relatively young and very able man—without work is a dangerous one and, furthermore, I—'

'You mystify me. Not only do you want to set up in some hermitage in the mountains but now you want me to leave my retirement and . . . are you truly suggesting I should *work*?'

'I suspected this solution would offend your delicate Venetian sensibilities, my love, but, yes, I am *suggesting that you work*. If your days have a structure, so can mine. As things are now, writing time is made of crumbs. Of whatever is left over. Besides, who knows if the books can continue to sufficiently provide—'

'Sufficiently provide for *you*—to fund wanderlust and trunkloads of fabric . . . month-long stays in Paris . . . 110,000 *lire* last month at Emilio's just for cheese . . .'

We're inside the ballroom now, sitting side by side on the sofa, all the better not to look one another in the eye. I say, 'You will recall that you, too, are fond of cheese, that we stay months at a time in Paris *together* and that the very napkin with which you pat your beautiful mouth was stitched from one of those metres of fabric, as were your sheets and—'

'As was that ridiculous dress you're wearing . . .'

'Ridiculous? How is it suddenly ridiculous? It's not so different from any other of my dresses.'

'Maybe it's not the dress. The dress itself is . . . it suits you. But not with those boots. It's the boots which are ridiculous. I prefer it when you wear sandals. How many pairs of sandals do you have with all those straps and ribbons?'

'I wear the boots for comfort during the four or five or more kilometres we walk over the cobblestones of this town each day, let alone those we walk in the hills.'

'Then wear gym shoes like other American women do.'

'I have never worn gym shoes. I wore pink ballet slippers with elastic bands across my instep even when I played field hockey at school.'

'You never played field hockey anywhere.'

'I did. Twice. I borrowed a stick and a puck and practised shushing about alone in the bathroom. I decided it wasn't a game for me. In any case, I shall never wear gym shoes—it's a matter of psychological comfort. I feel like a duck in gym shoes.'

'You look like a partisan in your boots.'

'I prefer partisan to duck.'

'I said *partisan*, not *partridge*.'

I get up to pace the room. Over my shoulder I say, 'I heard very well what you said and I still prefer partisan to duck. It's one thing to take on the responsibility of keeping us—that I have done, would continue to do as best

I can for all time—but when you add your requirements for more attention, when you resent the hours, count them, pace like a randy beast before the door to the studio, when you are irritated if I stop to speak to a reader or . . . It's as though you'd have me be an anonymous failure who somehow manages to earn splendid sums of money. You are essentially phlegmatic and you want me to be phlegmatic *with* you, as long as, sometime in the middle of the night and without insinuating upon our collective phlegmaticism, I shall continue to write books that sell. None of that is fair, Fernando. You've demanded that I be accountable and that makes me feel throttled. Yes, that's it. I feel *throttled.*'

'What does it mean, *trott-led?*'

'Jesus. Never mind. It only means that I'm tired.'

'*Trott-led.* I have never heard this word for *tired.*'

Suddenly the absurdity of our warring smashes through whatever anger I felt and I look at him for the first time. I see his perplexity. We have been speaking in English, a rare occurrence between us, inserting an Italian word only every now and then. I know how it feels to try to be understood in a language that is not one's own. I also know that every time one of us misplaces his humility, it's a signal for the other one to take aim.

I smile at him, move closer to him. 'That's not what it means at all. I can't explain right now what it means.'

Pulling me closer yet, pushing my head under his chin, very softly he says, 'Because you are too tired? Or because I am phlegmatic? I don't understand you.'

'Nor I you. That's the beauty of it, isn't it? At least we have two languages to blame. For our not understanding each other. I feel sad for couples who must manage without such a convenient rationale.'

The balcony doors are open to the April night and he goes to stand there. Can it be by accident that he stands in the single shaft of gold light gleaming from the lantern on the wall below in the *vicolo* Signorelli? He grips the iron railing in both hands, tilts his chin upward. A brooding Shylock ploughing the seas. I move closer to him, stop just inside the doors.

'You're not so much phlegmatic as you are Italian. Worse—Venetian. You're being yourself. You have never, not for an hour, been anyone but yourself. Your magnificent self. Your more than and less than magnificent selves. Me? You're right, I *am* behaving the fragile artist.'

He turns at that, leans elbows against the railing, settles his gaze somewhere above mine, holds his cigarette between thumb and forefinger, a 1930s German film star exhaling through his teeth.

Reverting to Italian, I say, 'Someone once said, *A writer is an expatriate no matter where she lives.* Maybe it was me. And maybe it's not so easy for you to live with an expatriate twice over. With the writer who, by very dint of being one, must often stay emotionally *apart*. With the foreigner who, by very dint of her *otherness*, must always be just a little bit separate.'

'You may be *separate*, as you call it, from this culture but you are not separate from me and I do understand better now that you require a particular kind of . . . I'll help you, we'll readjust our time so that there's no need for you to . . .' He's holding me close against the roughness of his Donegal vest and I love the espresso-and-red-wine-and-cigarette Italian man smell of him. He says, 'We've never spent a night apart since you came to live in Venice. Not one.'

'And during all the nights and days of those nine years, we've pretty much mapped out our lives according to your needs. From the beginning. From the first day I knew it would be that way. That you would lead. I understood that and it was fine with me. I was already full. It's still fine. Mostly fine. It's just that, for right now I have a need of my own. To stay apart for a time and work. Finish this book. I am not in revolt. I love the steps to our dance. I always have. Just for a while, I want to stay alone in Biagio's little house in the woods.'

CHAPTER II

Two days later—with Biagio perched on the edge of our back seat—we follow Neddo as he careens Biagio's old black Ford along the serpentine roads of the Lunigiana in western Tuscany. Volcanic hills cleaved by steep gorges, secreted high hamlets hung from craggy slopes, it feels a land forsaken and always more as we ascend the hostile heaped-up spires of the alps. Nearly three hours pass and even Biagio's gentle patter has gone quiet. A quick right onto a trodden-earth road through a wood of pines and spruce and we arrive. At least, we have stopped behind where Neddo has stopped. Trail's end. No house is visible. Fernando alternately grinds his teeth and speaks *sotto voce* oaths and I will be merry at all costs.

On foot, Biagio and Neddo lead the way downward and deeper into the wood, which looks more like Norway than Tuscany. A slash of blue water crashes just below the path. Cicadas thrum. The trees shiver in the thin silver breeze and make a greenish twilight of noon, the shadows all the more luscious for the stripes of powdery sun falling through the leaves. Our boots crunching over dried rust-red needles and tufts of wild sage, three of us are laughing, children on a lark. And then I see it.

Not so small, the house is square and made of large round stones. Steeply peaked, the roof is dark blue shale. Branches of lilac are fixed behind a great brass boar's head on a double door, green paint clinging in the crevices of its decaying wood, and on either side of it two windows, long and narrow, are covered with glossy black shutters.

'I discarded my renovation program after the shutters. They look like shiny sores against the stones, don't they? My father's father built the place. For the de Gaspari. It was the way of things then for gentlemen to have a place inviolate.' As though distracted by something, Biagio looks away, his face contorted. In an instant he recovers, and smiling too broadly asks, '*Carina come casina boscosa, no?* It's a fine little house in the woods, no?'

He pushes open the door, stands back. '*Avanti, avanti.* Ah, before I forget,' he points to the lilac on the old green door, 'there is one thing I would ask of you, that is to change the flowers on the door each day. I do most times, and Giorgia does, but I think it would be nice for you to do it while you're here. I've noticed you always have flowers or branches or the like on your door and . . .'

'I would like to do that, Biagino.'

'When the lilac and the forsythia are finished, the ginestra is blooming and then there are peach and plum blossoms, but if you prefer wildflowers . . . In autumn I mix yellow oak leaves and red berries; in winter, pine branches, but my favourite is to fix a length of vine still hung with bunches of grapes on the morning of the harvest. I like that the best but as I said, anything you'd . . .' He sweeps his arm in invitation.

A single room perhaps forty, fifty metres square, its air drenched in must and smoke and wine; the walls are stuccoed, the ceiling low and beamed in blackened oak. Hanging from the end of a thick, tape-wrapped wire which swings from one of the beams there is a tiny lightbulb. Biagio flips the switch which ignites it.

'*Ecco, Venere*—behold, Venus,' he says, grinning up at the bulb.

High and deep enough to sleep in and fitted with a chain-geared iron rotisserie on which an elk might rotate, the hearth is swept, logs readied. The floor is shale dug into earth, and tendrils of small blue bravehearts push up between the stones nearest the door. On a plank table there is a green glass bottle for oil, a pitcher for wine, an iron candle holder. One can imagine old hunters sitting on the seven chairs with their cups and their kill to sing and to weep. An open cupboard is painted green and sags under a motley store of dishes and glasses. Wood is everywhere piled in the most precise stacks, and bushels of kindling wait along the hearth stones. Large and dizzyingly ornate, a brass bed piled with three mattresses sits snug against one whitewashed wall, linens and quilts folded neatly upon its middle. On a nightstand sits a vase stuck with a small branch of pine. A two-step stool waits near the bed.

'You tell me I'm the true *princess and the pea*—finally I've found my rightful bed,' I say over my shoulder to

Fernando, who patrols the space with his gaze from the doorway. 'It's wonderful, don't you think? Austere. Ascetic.'

Biagio is asking Neddo, *Chi è questa principessa?* and Fernando wants to know, 'Did you check for nails under the mattress cover?'

Biagio pulls aside a green oilcloth curtain suspended from an iron semicircle to reveal a stone sink and a gas ring. A dollhouse fridge is cantilevered out on wooden stilts. On a butcher's block hung with knives there is a copper *paiuolo* and a jar of wooden spoons. Biagio runs to the far side of the room. *'Ecco il bagno.* Behold the bath.'

Though hung with the same green oilcloth, this time the rod is circular and the curtain reveals a sloping cement floor with a drain at its centre, a hand-held showerhead, a WC and another, smaller stone sink. Hung obliquely from wires is an enormous Campari Soda mirror, its tilt so extreme as to give view only of one's lower body. Having finished the tour, Biagio works on the fire, Neddo pours wine, Fernando resumes the *sotto voce* oaths.

'All that money to fix up the ballroom, why didn't you tell me what you really wanted was to play Spartacus and Sura . . . Did you bring chains?' He blows smoke in my face.

I take his hand, pull him out the door and we walk back down to the path by the creek, its hissing seeming louder now without the laughter. A woman—stoutly made and of a certain age, her dress dark and printed with yellow flowers, a fresh white kerchief covering her hair and knotted at the nape of her neck—manoeuvres up the path, a cloth-covered basket riding on her hip.

'Ah, *buongiorno, buongiorno . . . sono* Giorgia, *la moglia di* Biagio—I am Giorgia, Biagio's wife,' she says, laughing, setting down the basket to shake our hands. 'I've brought a little snack but whatever you might need, you must only ask. I'm embarrassed for that house.'

Eyes silvery-black like coal, sun-browned skin tight over a strong square jaw: I can see Neddo's face in his sister's. Fernando picks up the basket, takes Giorgia's arm and we walk back towards the house.

'*Signora* Giorgia, you are so kind and I appreciate your offer but I will be living very simply,' I explain. I know I must set boundaries now or I will fall into relying on this Giorgia. How easy that would be.

'*Si, si,* Biagio *e* Neddo, *loro mi hanno detto, ma* . . . Yes, yes, Biagio and Neddo, they've told me but . . .'

Giorgia unpacks her basket, trades chides with her husband and her brother, and begins to make up the bed; I help her. The men have laid out bread and prosciutto, yellow pears and a half-round of pecorino. As though to be separate from the men, Giorgia and I sit on the bed with our plates, she still apologising, mortified, she says, that a guest will be living in this *casa diroccata*, run-down house. Between slices of pear taken from the point of the clasp knife she wears on a string tied to the belt of her dress she lists my alternatives: her house, her sister's house in the village, the *mansarda* at Castelletto. Talking, laughing, rolling her eyes, relishing her pear, Giorgia makes the scene feel familiar. Like a homecoming might feel.

Giorgia orders the two men about, shepherding them out to the truck, telling them she'd rather walk than ride home, warning them about not drinking any more until supper, saying lettuces and the last of the asparagus need to be picked.

The plates and glasses all washed and back on their shelves, the princess bed tucked and fluffed, my workplace set up, a candle lit, Fernando sits on his haunches by the fire, poking it. Quietly he says, 'I still can't understand why we're doing this.'

'Please. We've talked and talked about it all. I am not staying here because I don't want to be with you but because I *do* want to be peaceful with my work. I need, very sorely *need* to finish this book and what with the workmen crashing about and the season beginning in Orvieto . . . but you *know* all of this.'

'Yes, I know all of this.'

I go to sit on the floor next to him. 'You'll be fine, you'll—'

'I *will* be fine. The men will be at work in the *salone* and I will be there with them. And Barlozzo has claimed two days a week of my time. The guest room needs some work after Emily's nocturnal adjusting of the armoires and the bookcases. It needed another coat of old Bordeaux anyway. I trust Neddo will look in on me. I'm already overbooked. And I'll leave Orvieto on Friday mornings, be here in time to take you to lunch. We'll have two and a half days for us.'

'Maybe not that much. We'll see. I would love to wander about these little villages. We could spend some time in the Garfagnana . . .'

'I counted on the resurgence of your wanderlust. I'll plan little *gitarelle* for us, book us into nice little places each Saturday night.'

'Wonderful. Now, please, it's time to go. The longer you stay . . . it won't get easier . . .'

I'm reading when a rapping on the door—soft, insistent—distracts me. It's Giorgia with her basket, I know it is. Another blanket. A jug of hot milk and brandy. I must try again to convince her . . .

'I didn't want to frighten you. You see, I was just passing by . . .' His blueberry eyes are sparklers, triumphal in the gathering dusk.

'I knew you wouldn't leave.'

He holds me, kisses me close to my ear, asks, 'Did you really want me to?'

'Yes. And no.'

'I heard the no.'

'Fernando, please don't . . .' I push him away. Gently and not *so* far away.

'I *will* leave. I will leave this place. Let you be. Let you work. But that doesn't mean I have to go all the way back to Orvieto. I've been up to Biagio and Giorgia's place. Biagio says it would be helpful to him if I spent my days with him. Neddo's going to stay, too. At least for a while. And Neddo called Barlozzo, said he should come up, too. I think he will. Giorgia is keen, has a list of . . .'

'This was supposed to be a retreat and you're turning it into a Toscanaccio jamboree.'

'I am not Tuscan and neither is Neddo. And it's not a jamboree at all that we have in mind. We're going to work. Giorgia will see to it. If you'll just think about it, it's a perfect plan. Everyone wins.'

'You don't even have a pair of socks.'

'Five or six pairs, actually . . . a small bag . . . on the off-chance that—'

'I'm not going to cook. Bread, oil, wine. A pot of beans. Maybe a pot of beans.'

'I won't even be here. You'll eat what you want. We can go into the village in the evenings for supper. This place will feel very small after a day of work.'

'Please don't decide how things will feel for me.'

'*Giusto*, fair.' He nods. 'My days at work with the *ragazzi*, yours with the book. Evenings together. Let's just try it. I promise to leave if that's what you still want after a two-day trial. Just two days, that's all I ask.'

'Sunrise to sunset, no contact.'

'No contact. I'll take a walk now. Be back after the sun sets.'

'Which will be in about four minutes.'

CHAPTER III

I work and I walk. I eat when I'm hungry and sleep a happy child's sleep. A day-by-day solitude I have never lived. I thrive. But if there was no Fernando, no great, soul-wrenching love in my life, would this same solitude feel like loneliness? I think it would. I think he's the luxury that makes this bliss. I write a note to tell him so. And to tell him that a Thursday has never seemed so long. Today is Thursday. I put the note under the pillow on his side of the bed. Tomorrow evening he will be here.

Saving me the dread task, it was Giorgia who, last Sunday, disengaged the 'work committee', sent Biagio back to his duties, Neddo and Fernando back to Orvieto. Having summarily declined to join them, Barlozzo had stayed at home. I imagine his response when Fernando telephoned him. *Let her be.*

Hair slicked with lime-perfumed gel and parted in the middle, moustaches clipped, his old leather bomber slung on a shoulder, my consort—bearing gifts—lopes down the path on Friday afternoon. I wait for him. Cautious, timid while the four days' separation falls away, we court each other. He brings neroli oil and cinnamon candles. After cooling it in the creek, I pour his prosecco down the slant of the rose-coloured Venetian *calice* I found in the village *antiquario.* Hand him a bowl of wild strawberries smaller than a baby's fingernail. The windows flung, the shutters tapping on the stone, we lie on the princess bed, limbs about limbs, and watch the dark creep in. Someone from Castelletto trots a horse up the creek path sending the young boar on their evening's *passeggiata* dartling back into the woods. I read passages from the text and he tells me news, what he's cooked, how he feels. He says that Neddo has moved into the guest room at number 34 and feels quite grand, plays *maggiordomo* when Barlozzo comes to visit. Fernando is, I think, both grateful for my peace and jealous of it. How two-faced is love. His and mine.

After a long morning session at work, I pack bread and wine and bits of Giorgia's gifts into the vintage Prada backpack and set off into the hills. How many feasts in how many places have been tucked into this old black bag? I walk until I find the right place to sit. A long draught of the cold wine, a rip at the bread, a genteel gorge under a two o'clock slant of May Tuscan light. Another kind of light. Another kind of Tuscany.

No chaste watercolour land this one. No zigzag of cypress strutting a green velvet meadow, no yellow pasture cascading, *dolcemente*, to the horizon. Not a single red-roofed hilltown heaped in the saddle of some telluric outcrop, here the Tyrrhenian Sea moans at the feet of sheer shale cliffs and sheep drift like fallen clouds over the pastures of the high plateaus. In ruined castles on gorse-spiked hills, Shades bay like wolves, the locals say. Gaunt alpine crags make a half-broken gate around the land and it was here in the cleaved white hearts of them that Michelangelo strode in search of his stone. Another Tuscany this one.

Eight copper-coloured cows in a small pasture, a fallow field broken by an avenue of oaks, the trees retreating downward into the next wood. Locked with a chain, arched iron gates wound with wild roses stand alone in the middle of a meadow. What did they once open upon? Who was it they shut out? Short, squat olives and old vines line the verges of the white road and in the ditches there are nettles and flowers whose names I don't know and don't need to. Yellow, blue mostly. Purple. Brambles. On my own I am. Like the child who would escape—bread and jam in a pocket—to sleep under the dining room table. Solitude untethered by love is loneliness, I understand that now. I walk fast and then sit. Lie in prickly grass, count three faint chimes of the bell at San Agostino. Somewhere a creek crashes and blackbirds screech in a measured tattoo. In broad orange letters a sign promises *Vino e olio vendita diretta*. Wine and oil for sale. A kind of

Tuscan lemonade stand. I had one once. Not Tuscan and not in the countryside but on the cement walk in front of Maria's wooden house on Warren Street. 408.

The girls across the way had set up for enterprise. Annie and Doreen they were, ten and eleven to my eight. Far older was their sister Marion, who wore a cotton dress with a small lace collar and lipstick which she kept in her pocket and applied while looking in the side mirror of Buonome's van which was always parked half on the sidewalk. Fifteen I think she was. It was she, Marion, who marked me. Set me on the path to painted lips. I wanted her dress and her flat white leather shoes with the drawstrings tied in bows just below where her toes began. More I wanted that silvery tube. Now I pat the Russian Red safe in my pocket. *Lemonade, a nickel*, read Annie and Doreen's sign in cursive letters. If I could earn my keep, maybe I wouldn't have to go back. Maybe Maria would let me stay.

A wooden crate from the coffee lady up on Jay Street, my stand was smaller than theirs. *Iced lemonade, two cups for 10 cents.* Maria's pitcher was glass, round and squat with cherries painted on the side. I used brown sugar instead of white and had to stir hard. The cherries on the pitcher sprung an idea. *May I please have the jar of maraschinos in the fridge?* A new sign: *Iced lemonade with a cherry, two cups for 10 cents.* An early gastronomic success. Still I had to go back. Still I am trying to earn my keep. My keep, my place, my balance. I'd tried to be so good at Maria's, almost invisible, to have no needs of my own, to earn my way into her heart. By selling lemonade, by trying to make her happy. When, after I'd known him only a few days, Fernando asked me to marry him, I was very much that same eager-to-please eight-year-old. Even at that early point, Fernando's needs and wants were clear as rainwashed air. I told myself, *The only way this will work is if I go to Venice with very few needs of my own. Another kind of invisibility. Fernando must lead. And not because he has always led but because he never has.* No mincing through a minefield, no painted-on pleasantness, it's only that, between the two of us, I am the one who is already *full*. No. I'm the one who is already full *enough*.

They must be the daughters, I think. It's late afternoon on a day when I've worked nearly straight through and so have saved my walk to the village for now. Tall, slender, arms linked, two women stroll a few paces ahead. One in jeans and brogues, grey-brown hair scraped back into a ponytail, the other in a long brown dress, the same grey-brown hair caught in a chignon and fixed casually with tortoiseshell pins, they stop at the *caffè* where I, too, am headed. As they enter, the barista steps from behind his post; a restrained bow first to the chignon, then to the ponytail. Waving him away and laughing, the two exchange greetings with everyone in the small, narrow room. They seat themselves and still I've not seen their faces, though, in truth, how could I know if they were kin to Biagio's Antonia? In the outlander's common pose of nonchalance, I am waiting my turn at the bar when the ponytail turns towards me in her chair, smiles broadly, rises, her hands outstretched—palms up—as to a long-lost friend.

'You must be Marlena. I'm Antonia's daughter. Filippa. Come to join us, won't you. Will you take tea?'

'Thank you so much but I, I'm—'

'I know, I know. Biagio has given us the word, both he and Giorgia have taken on your privacy as a mission. We're not to drop in or in any way disturb you, but since you're here and . . .' Only a metre away, she stands, pulls me towards their table. 'Antonia, I present Marlena. Marlena, this is Antonia.'

Antonia? This is Biagino's famous Antonia? Startlingly beautiful, it's true. Straight, thick, still-dark brows showing off those eyes. Antonia is already talking to another woman. Two others in fact, one who has taken a chair at the table and one who stands leaning over her, speaking in quiet tones.

Antonia tilts her face up to me. 'Ah, *l'Americana.*'

If a cold fish could speak, it would have her voice. Saying nothing more, she returns her attentions to the others and Filippa shuffles me back to the bar, a warden hurrying along a vassal from an unsuccessful audience with the queen. 'I do hope you'll let us know should you need anything. You can always send a note up with Biagio or . . .'

'No, no, managing nicely . . . A good rhythm to the . . . So peaceful . . .' I can't seem to finish a sentence. Was Antonia as ungracious as I think she was?

'Lovely to meet you, Marlena,' Filippa is saying. 'Biagio and Giorgia have sung your praises. They feel so important . . . "a writer in residence".' She says this last in English.

'Yes, well, not such a . . .'

'Oh, and don't be put off by Antonia's reserve. Everyone who's not a local is always a little suspect. She's eighty-three and . . .'

Two sips of espresso and I'm out the door. Eighty-three? Seems more a nicely kept sixty. In any case, she seems curiously indolent for a zealot . . . Beautiful, yes, but the way she said, *Ah, l'Americana* . . . And why in the world would Filippa—who if her mother is eighty-three must herself be sixty-something—introduce herself as Antonia's daughter?

By chance, by design, Filippa is often on the path by the creek in the late mornings, she ambling down as I climb. Sometimes I see her sitting, reading or gathering the cress-like leaves which sprout along the verges. We wave, nod, wish each other a good day. Nothing more. It's been two, perhaps three weeks of these passing greetings when one morning she asks if I've found the stone benches at the top of the path. I have.

'Would you like to sit for a while?' she asks.

'I would.'

'Your work, does it go well?'

'Oh, yes. I'm . . .'

'I've been wanting to apologise to you. For Antonia's rudeness. She—'

'It did startle me, her *indifference*, though my first encounters with many Orvietani were much the same. No need to . . . I was a bit disenchanted, though, since Biagio has always spoken of her so worshipfully . . .'

'Yes. His first love, I think. He was nine years old when Antonia came to live at Castelletto. Antonia was seventeen. She's kept him beguiled ever since. But then again, everyone does. Love her. Everyone who doesn't—'

'May I invite you to an early lunch?' Desiring to turn our talk away from Antonia, I pull bread from my pack. A sack of cherries. Cheese. I begin to tear the bread, and from her jeans pocket Filippa pulls out the knife I've seen her use to cut wild grasses. Divides up the small wedge of pecorino.

'I've got wine in a flask if you'd like,' I offer.

'No, this is fine. You're not German, by the way, are you? I mean, Americans always have such complex backgrounds, half this, half . . .'

A rather strange non sequitur, her question. I can only laugh, shake my head before I say, 'No, not German. Not that I know. But why would . . . ?'

'I ask only because . . . well, Antonia suffers from old war wounds, one physical, many more emotional. My stepfather and one of my grandfathers were in the Resistance. From what I understand they *were* the Resistance in these parts. I was five or six. I recall almost nothing . . .'

'And so for Antonia, it still rages. The war.'

'Not that it rages, but she is of the *ancien régime*. Rigid territorial ideas . . . She remains sensitive to any form of *occupation*. By that I mean she disapproves of strangers who want a piece of Tuscany to call their own.'

'Not just Germans, then. Americans, too.'

'Yes, and the English, the Dutch, even other Italians. It's the Germans, though, for whom she saves her purest rancour.'

'Rigid, yes, quite . . . Italians as well?'

'Antonia doesn't consider herself Italian. She is Tuscan. The rest of Italy is only a land mass which surrounds Tuscany. I can assure you I barely enlarge upon the facts as she sees them.'

'And so is it that all we *others* are interlopers?'

'Oh, yes. According to Antonia, yes. And as she grows older her sentiments take on an always stronger voice. Or perhaps it's that she less and less feels the need to censor them. Surely her opinions have been conditioned by the time she spends each year with de Gaspari cousins in another part of Tuscany. Between Pienza and Montepulciano. Do you know that area?'

'We lived for two years in San Casciano dei Bagni. That area was our greater garden.'

'Well then, you might begin to understand.'

'Not really.'

'So many of the old *casolari* have been bought up by strangers. Flats in the villages as well. Mostly Germans and Americans. Some Dutch.'

'But that's true in so many areas of Tuscany and Umbria. Lately Poles and Russians have joined the ranks, and Brazilians, Argentines . . .'

'I wouldn't mention that to Antonia. In any case, it's the Germans who are the stinging thorns, while the English and the Americans are assigned the status of irritant. Her name for the Germans is far too inelegant to repeat. Her most temperate name for the English and the Americans is *colonists*. Accurate enough, wouldn't you say? After all, they do tend to set up together, speak only their own language, lament the dearth of marmalade and cheddar cheese, a decent hamburger, are annoyed that all the *trattorie* cook the same foods—*cured meats and those little bread things with oil and tomatoes, pasta, pasta, pasta, pork chops, sausages, wild boar, those yucky pigeons, immense still-bleeding beefsteaks. And panna cotta from a box and too-sweet jam tarts . . . I can bake a better pie.* They want to come here because it's different and then set about to make the place over in the image of whence they came.'

Filippa is spirited. Her barbs are sharp, her American twang correctly nasal. It's a good thing I'm not itching to have a word, though, since she leaves scant space between accusations. Now she is saying, 'And there's a sort of Edwardian stance among them, the Americans especially. They buy the ruin, snap their fingers to call up a retinue of courtiers to do their bidding: masons, plumbers, electricians, marble workers, painters, gardeners, cooks, housekeepers, their own personal cast of adorable peasants.'

Her American voice at work again, she recites a two-person dialogue:

Don't you just love Giacinto and Giuseppe? Even if they do smell and . . .

And what about those teeth . . .

Yes, all two of them sticking up like . . .

I wonder how they're able to . . .

I know, I wonder, too . . .

But they are dear . . .

Dear, yes, but still one must watch every move they make . . .

I know, I know. All peasants steal. It's in their blood.

My Charlie's right. Best we all stick together.

Oh my god, isn't that the truth.

Filippa laughs, pleased with her burlesque, and I'm laughing with her, shaking my head and recalling the nearly verbatim indictments I've heard myself over the years. She has more to say.

'The strange thing is that foreigners either don't know or pretend not to know or care what the locals say and think and, sometimes, what curse they call down on them. They really believe that if a local does more than wish them a good day, he's embraced them as family. If they only knew. They mistake for affection the peasant's intrinsic impulse to "patronise". Hands on his hips, eyes twinkling, when a peasant greets a stranger with compliments and good wishes, he's most likely performing. We are a race of actors but the peasants are more skilful artists than the rest of us. All that's between a local and an outsider is economics. And mutual mistrust.'

'Much of the world turns by the force of mutual mistrust. Italy has no monopoly on that commodity. But what about the strangers who come to Italy and work for years and years to restore not only an abandoned house but fallow lands which the Tuscans themselves left behind after the war, all those who traded a sharecropper's misery for that of a factory worker? What about the ones who—'

'Yes, yes, but they do it for fun . . . for a romp. They fancy themselves gentlemen farmers and prance like barons because they've squeezed eight litres of oil out of their trees and then go on to display it like an art project. *Have you, like, seen Jack's oil?*' Back to screeching in an American twang.

'And to which circle of hell do you assign the foreigners who have lived here for the best years of their lives, the ones who . . . ?'

'Do you mean those who, having surrendered all else, come here because it's the only place in the world where they want to be? The ones with no other house in Frankfurt or Los Angeles or some little village near Amsterdam? The ones who embrace the community and live the life the locals live? These are another class. Rare. More exiles than expatriates. We are not speaking of them.'

'I see.' Of course I don't see at all.

Filippa pulls off the elastic which holds back her hair, scrapes the curly mass of it higher on her head, resecures the elastic. I look at her, try to find what I can recall of her mother's face in hers. Antonia's is heart-shaped with a flat, broad forehead, cheekbones high and sharp, a pointed chin. A nose long and slender, all the better for sneering. Filippa's is a *faccia piena*, a full face, the Antonia-bones softened. Her long blue eyes, pale as ice on a northern lake, those are Antonia's.

As though she's only just noticed she's been lampooning Americans in the face of one, Filippa stops, flutters her hands. 'I hope, I mean, you understand that all this is not meant for, not for *you*, of course. You're married to an Italian, you're—'

'It's okay. Really. Yours is the insider's take. I've heard it before. From the Venetians, the San Cascianesi, from the Orvietani. Proposed, though, with—what shall I call it?—a lesser *hostility*.'

'I . . . well, I was only . . .'

'I'm not offended. Nor do I disagree with many of your impressions.'

'Where do you stand then? With the outsiders? With the locals?'

'Mostly by myself. I've never been much good at playing the expatriate. I tend to chime in with the local chorus wherever I am, all the while being aware that I am not and never can become a *local* myself. I'm quite content belonging nowhere. Or is it everywhere? I can never decide.'

Filippa looks at me, looks down almost as though she is embarrassed for me. I can hear her thinking, *poveretta.* To a fourth- or fifth-generation Tuscan—or is she sixth generation?—I am surely an aberration. I am to most people. *Where* is *your real home? Don't you miss* home?

'Belonging nowhere or everywhere is not the same as being vagabondish, *footloose and fancy free.* Walls and windows raised up on a certain patch of earth can be marvellous and I've loved all of mine but why would I restrict myself to those? It's the home inside me I can't live without.'

'The home inside? Do you mean . . . ?'

'The "moveable feast", the peace that travels where I do. Self-trust. I've been working on it brick by brick since I was a child.'

Filippa bends to pull a silver cigarette case from the pocket of the tweed jacket she'd removed and let fall among the weeds and wildflowers. She offers it to me and I shake my head. We gaze at each other closely as she pulls a match across a tiny red box of them. She smiles and, leaning her head back to rest upon the oak trunk behind her, inhales deeply. Hungry for the smoke, she gulps it, blows out in tiny ragged wisps what little she didn't swallow. She looks at me.

'You sound so much like Antonia,' she says.

'You'll pardon me, but I dearly hope . . .'

'Oh no, I don't mean that side you saw of her in the village, not that. You're so, so *self-contained*. I suspect you're whole-hearted the way she is, you know, all or nothing at all. And you're mysterious the way she is. The way you said, *I'm quite content belonging nowhere*. That's something Antonia would say. No further illumination. What was the film? *Five Easy Pieces*. Five pithy words. Full stop. Even when Antonia is grandiloquent, ranting or preaching, remembering, even then one senses she leaves off just at the best part. The worst part.'

One of my own tricks. *Conversational coitus interruptus*, someone once called it. *You tease*, he'd said. Another one said, *You speak in aliases but I know that every one of the characters is you.*

The wind rises, and the high grasses stoop nearly to the ground, stay there swaying for a beat or two then stand again, bend again; flowers with long yellow petals dance among them, their heads in a petulant toss. I tell her, 'It's true, I write more easily than I speak.'

'Yes, well, that's likely made things easier for you then, living among this race of orators.'

'I suppose it has.'

'So you're *content belonging nowhere* and Antonia is content *only belonging in Tuscany*. And only surrounded with other Tuscans. But there are others in the family would just as soon sell off some of the land, a few of the unused buildings, or perhaps transform part of Castelletto into a kind of tourist retreat. A resort. Lodgings, restaurants. Perhaps a golf course. A swimming pool or two. Even talk of it sends Antonia on a holy rampage.'

'I wouldn't have thought there would be a significant population of strangers banging on the doors of the estate agents here. Or that it would attract any but the heartiest tourists. Wonderful as it is, it hardly fits the Italy-dreamers' image of Tuscany.'

'That's the crux. That other Tuscany is running out of properties. Umbria used to be called "the next Tuscany" and you, living where you do, must admit the seers were right. There are those who say our part of Tuscany is next.'

'So your fear, Antonia's fear, of "occupation" is, as yet, theoretical.'

'Theoretical, yes. But, as I said, some of the family want to hurry the process. There's a rift among us, wide and, I think, impassable.'

'I think a family of one is the only family without a rift. And, even then, not always. And yours, how many of you are there?'

'It depends on who you're asking. Antonia says there are seven of us. Seven plus Biagio and Giorgia. In a way she's right. Our men—husbands, lovers, companions— they've come and gone over the years. My Umberto is the only one who's been a constant. Antonia insists that my forty-three years of marriage to him is not yet sufficient

to grant him full family status. And he's a de Gaspari.
A third cousin. We were introduced at a wedding when
he was sixteen and I was twelve.'

She wants to tell me more and my smile invites her.
I like this Filippa better, her mocking voice gone liques-
cent. Unbinding her hair, she is twelve again.

'Even then we knew what the tittering was all about.
Each of us docile in our own way, we let them scheme
and pinch our cheeks and roll their eyes. And calculate
what each side would be gaining by the match.'

'And that was that?'

'At some point we really did fall in love. I don't recall
if it was at another wedding or maybe a funeral. Some
prescribed family gathering. I know I was seventeen and he
about to be *laureato* when he began to visit at Castelletto.
He brought his father once and the three men—Umberto,
his father and Ugo, my stepfather—spent endless hours
hunting or riding, sauntering back up the oak walk all
flushed and rosy, voices ringing, arms linked. Needs
linked. His mother's ruby ring slid down to my lips with
the last sip of red wine at dinner one evening, everyone
at table but me knowing of Umberto's surprise. Yes,
I think we really were in love, Umberto and I. After all

these years we agree on most things, we're easy with each other. We laugh a good deal. Having never longed for a great consuming sort of love, Umberto is all the love I've ever needed. Sometimes I do wonder what it would feel like, though. That other kind of love. I should think it would be frightening.' She looks away, says this last more to herself than to me.

Turning her gaze back to me she says, 'Umberto, my sister Luce and I look after the farms. The commercial parts. The marketing of oil and wine, lately of cheese. Other crops. Our work seeps more and more into what was once Biagio's authority. Officially Biagio remains *fattore* but, over the years, we and a small group of others support him. Antonia sees to the sacredness of Biagio's sense of propriety. *Guai a chi lo tocca*: wrath to he who touches it. She and Biagio are . . . well, they have a long history together. *Amici del cuore*, heart friends, one would defend and protect the other to the death.'

'You said he was only a little boy when Antonia . . .'

'Yes, a little boy born old, born wise.'

'So there are you and Luce . . . ?'

'Maria-Luce. Mary-Light. She is named after my paternal grandmother. From the stories Biagio and

Antonia tell about her, the first Maria-Luce and Antonia were inseparable. She died soon after my father did. When I was an infant.'

'Just the two of you then, you and your sister, no other . . . ?'

'No. Just Luce and me. You've not met her yet, have you? She's mentioned that she plans to come down to greet you; she's only just returned from America. Meetings with importers . . . wine and oil, some other of our products.'

'Is she . . . are you alike?'

'Not so much. Physically we are much the same but our characters are not. Luce is bright, extroverted, perfect for the role of Castelletto emissary to the greater world. I prefer backstage.'

'Is she married?'

'She was. In her second year at university in Bologna, she had a romance with a medical student, Pietro Beneventano da Siracusa—noble Sicilian lineage, thin pockets. They married one Saturday morning in the Bologna city hall, changed clothes, set to the task of transferring Pietro's belongings into the flat Luce shared with a fellow architecture student before heading off to L'Osteria del Sole to drink with their friends. Luce informed Antonia via telegram. Antonia and I—I think Umberto was with us—had met Pietro when we'd visited Luce a few months earlier. Antonia pronounced him *una creatura simpatica*, marvelled at his eyes . . . *petrolio*, she called their colour, black with shards of green and silver. *As though the Arabs and the Normans are still fighting it out in those great black pools*, she'd said.

'But from then on Luce had only mentioned Pietro in passing, never invited him to Castelletto, seemed pleased to see her old beaux when she visited on holidays, and so the news of her marriage to Pietro was shocking. After Sabina was born and they'd separated, it was Pietro who came to visit, he who explained to Antonia that they'd married only to legitimise their child. Antonia and Ugo—Luce's father, my stepfather—offered to raise Sabina at Castelletto while Luce finished her studies, but Luce—declining even an increased allowance—managed things herself. A larger flat, a live-in nanny; she would race back from classes to nurse Sabina, to play with her, wheel her about on campus or under the porticos of the old *palazzi*. Often she would tuck her in a sack strapped to her chest, take her to lectures. Having arranged the use of empty halls three times a week, she taught Italian conversation to a group of twenty or so foreign students, the pittance each one paid adding up to the sum of her rent. Luce never broke stride.'

Nor do you, I think. I am a prop on her Strindberg stage, saving her talking to the trees. To herself. Bootless by now and nearly supine on the stone bench, my sack as a pillow.

'My own little girls were then four and two. Viola the elder, Isotta the baby. Once a month or sometimes more, I would pack them up, drive to Bologna and we'd stay a few days with Luce and Sabina. With three babies under five, roaming the markets, cooking and cleaning and feeding and bathing, when all was finally quiet I'd lie on the sofa near Luce's desk and read half the night while she wrote her papers. Prone and facing away from her, I would sometimes raise an arm behind my head, thrust my hand out to her and, without words, without even taking her eyes from her work, she would reach out to hold it. Too, every once in a while Luce would come over to me, sit beside me, lean down to kiss me, say something akin to: *We could never do this if Mamma was here; she'd be running the show, marching us here and there* . . . Though I didn't agree with her, I said nothing. As though she'd had a mother different from mine, I never understood why she felt that way, why what was true for her was not always so for me. Not then, not yet, I didn't understand. By now, though, I do. My own girls—my Viola and Isotta—had different mothers. They still do. But how does it happen? Do we love one child more than another according to how they love us? Was Viola easier to love than Isotta because she was always so ardent in her love for *me*? Isn't love—all sorts of love—fanned or cooled by reciprocity? I think it is.'

'Or could it be that one child *feels* he's less loved than another and so becomes his own Home Guard, defending himself against the pain of that feeling? Or the pain of that truth? And so makes himself *harder to love*? It may begin with us. More likely it begins long before us. Some would say that pain is passed down like the slope of a cheek, the cut of the eyes. I don't believe that. I don't want to believe that.'

'That sounds like Antonia, too.' Filippa rubs a thumbnail across the rough stone of the bench, energetically smoothing its edge. She looks at the nail, rubs it again across the stone. 'Do you have children?'

'I have a son and a daughter. Both fine people, both embarked on their journeys, if somewhat disparate ones.'

'Disparate from yours or from each other?'

'Both.'

Filippa looks at me, waits for more. All she gets is my smile as I set about putting things back in my sack. I zip and unzip the pockets, rearrange things. I slide my thoughts away from my daughter. Not hiding, not pretending, I pull across my mind an old darkish curtain. Behind it her voice is still clear but not so close. *Mom, you've hurt me.* Let me count the ways. Of course I have. How I wish you could have known me when I was your age. Or when I was ten. I wanted the fairytale for you and maybe that was the way I hurt you most.

'Are you heading back already?' Filippa asks. 'Won't you stay a while more? It's the most beautiful hour of the afternoon now, don't you think? I can't remember the last time I had so much to say to anyone. Let me just finish up about Luce and then you'll be on your way . . . Let's see now . . .'

I want to stay and I want to leave and it's Filippa who decides for me, takes up her Strindberg.

'It was after she graduated that Luce brought Sabina home. After she'd demonstrated her independence, her possessiveness of her child . . . and then, well . . . Sabina is an extraordinary woman, by the way. Devoted to her mother *and* her grandmother, her chosen role is that of family peacemaker. Or was it that peacemaker was the only role no one else had taken on? She is married to Gianluca, a commander in the Navy and a professor at the Accademia Navale in Livorno. Gianluca lives in their flat there while she stays here smoothing the path between Luce and Antonia, and running the household with Giorgia. Gianluca joins her on the weekends. As I said, our men come and go.'

'And your daughters?'

'Viola is my elder. She's a beauty in much the same way that Antonia is. It's a fatal gift, I think. Their sort of beauty. The imperfect kind, the kind that lasts forever. She demonstrates Antonia's strengths, too, if in ways that are particularly her own. Antonia dotes on her, indulges her eccentricities. Viola went to school in France and stayed on to live there throughout her twenties, studying oenology and eventually apprenticing on a prestigious old estate in Bordeaux. She married the youngest son of the family. A fable, her wedding at sunset among the yellow-leafed, just-harvested vines under a pink and gold sky. She came home after three years. They've never officially divorced but . . . Having taken up the winemaking here, she's made a rather grand success of it, Viola has. The undisputed darling of the European wine journals, as I've said, she's a beauty.

'The de Gaspari flat in Firenze is where Viola lives during the winter, and Antonia and I are often with her there. With her and her companion, her long-time *fidanzato. Un vero* Fiorentino—a true Florentine patrician—he is older than she. Older, too, than I. Moving about among the dimmed glories of the old apartments, we four are good together, each one bent on the others' comfort. We spend our days as we will, though in the evenings we are together. Mostly at Frescobaldi. Raising a ruckus afterwards in the ghostly quiet of the Signoria, singing *"Che gelida manina"* under the loggia near Judith and Holofernes, we go to sit for the ritual cup of chocolate at Rivoire. Winter becomes Firenze, don't you think?

'Ah, yes, I was telling you of my Viola. She is happy in the way that women who have had more than one life can sometimes be happy. Having made them with resolve before regrets could have stained them, she is content with her decisions. She thrives. Not so Isotta.'

'Ah, Isotta?'

'An *avvocato*. An attorney who shares her practice and sometimes her life with Guglielmo. Though they keep a small studio in the village here—where Isotta conducts much of her part of the firm's affairs—their principal offices are in Genoa. Guglielmo keeps a flat there. Isotta says he also keeps a woman. Isotta shifts between despair and diffidence, finding solace first in one, then the other, never quite ready to devote herself to him. You see, when she was twenty, travelling with school friends, she fell in love with a Belgian. A married Belgian with whom she had a child. Magdalena is eighteen now. Though he has never again had a presence in her life—and never at all in their daughter's—one presumes Isotta has yet to recover from her Belgian. Understanding this, Guglielmo waits. He comes to Castelletto on most weekends. Apart from his *rapporto* with Isotta, Guglielmo is Antonia's *avvocato di fiducia*, her trusted attorney. His father, his grandfather were de Gaspari attorneys and so his connection to the family is historical. Antonia takes Guglielmo's part, calls Isotta fool. We did speak of rifts, yes? One might say that Isotta cultivates them. With Guglielmo, with her sister, with her daughter, with me. With Antonia.'

'And you . . . you with your sister? With Luce?'

'We try. Though Luce has always believed in Antonia's favouritism—her preference of me over her—we try. She and I. She and Antonia—despite Sabina's interventions—well, their mutual contempt is legend. And yet one can't live without the other. Luce is envious of Antonia. Of her beauty, her charm, of course. More, I think, of her courage. Antonia has always marched through life doing what had to be done. Mostly making it look easy. A daunting figure for a daughter to follow. And then there's that spell Antonia works on the world just by showing up. Waters part for her and I think they always will. A birthright; nothing like that comes to one by *aspiring* to it. I suppose when I was growing up I wished Antonia to be different than she was. Less *vivid*. More like other mothers. Luce has never stopped wishing for that. I think that's it. They remain in the classic struggle of the female adolescent and her mother. So many women do. Over time Luce seems to have fixed me along with Antonia inside her quite amiably executed intentions to punish as well as to revere. Antonia accepts both. Me? I accept neither. Luce has faded remarkably for me over the years so that sometimes I can hardly see her.'

Eyes closed, Filippa seems to have reached the end of Act I. Without speaking I pull on my boots, leave them untied, reach for my sack. Quietly I say, 'Filippa, I've enjoyed this time—'

But she's alert again, talking over my exit line. 'Must you go? I . . .'

'It's been lovely and, well, we've talked about so many things . . .'

'I've talked about so many things . . . such a patient listener . . .' She retrieves her jacket from where it had lain, brushes the grasses and blossoms from it, puts it on. 'I do apologise. Around here everyone already knows everything about everyone else or thinks they do, so I—well, it's not as though there is someone *new* very often.'

'Antonia sees to that, I'm sure.'

We laugh, she almost to tears. She reaches up to pluck a leaf from the oak behind the benches, brushes it along the blade of her knife. Puts it in the pocket of her jacket. I hold out my hand to her, turn and start down the path in a kind of shuffle since my left leg is all pins and needles, but she's still talking. Pretending not to hear, I turn to wave. She's running after me.

'I nearly forgot. You're invited to supper this evening. Command performance.'

'I, I'm not . . . you understand that . . . I mean, I hope your mother won't be offended but . . .'

'Amusing—the thought of Antonia being offended. She quite understands your intention to remain alone but she asks that you make this exception. I believe you've intrigued her. Or perhaps the *idea* of you has intrigued her.'

'Filippa, I can't . . .'

'*Va bene*. Should you change your mind, know that you'll be welcome. I think there'll be eleven of us tonight. Safety in numbers. *Buon lavoro*—good work.'

Taking a small purse from her jacket pocket she opens it, busies herself with its contents. Anything to avoid leaving. Abruptly she looks at me, leans towards me, puts a hand on my cheek. 'We dress for dinner, by the way. Antonia's choice.'

CHAPTER IV

Back at the lodge, I prop myself up on the princess bed, begin reading the morning's text. Trying to read it. How many of the seven lives of the seven women had Filippa recounted? I should have built a fire and brought a quilt. Another piece of cheese. I think how far Filippa strays from the typical Tuscan reserve and my head spins with estranged French husbands, Belgian lovers, arranged marriages, pink and gold skies, mothers and daughters, Florentine nobles, thorny Germans, Edwardian colonists. *Guglielmo keeps a flat there. Isotta says he also keeps a woman . . . There's a rift among us, wide and impassable.*

You sound so much like Antonia. We dress for dinner, by the way. Antonia's choice. I put the pages aside, slip out of my clothes and behind the green oilcloth curtain. A long shower. A good supper. *I think there'll be eleven of us tonight. Safety in numbers.*

It's not as though I changed my mind. That I reconsidered the invitation, *decided* to accept it. Rather it's that—even as I was declining—there was no question that I would be there. Filippa knew that before I did. Did she also know that, though I was startled by some of what she said, I *cheered her form*, rejoiced to hear an Italian expound upon what she has examined and reflected and concluded? For nine years now I have sat and stood for, strolled along to and lain down for discourses made of whimsy. Italians eat their own words. What is shouted and sworn over the *bruschette* and a few thin slices of *finocchiona* is recanted between the forkfuls of furled *pappardelle con funghi porcini* one carries to his genteelly open maw, disavowed as he skates a crust of bread in the winey juices of a *brasato* and—as he flicks away an errant speck of *zuppa inglese*

Antónia and her Daughters

from his chiselled chin with the tip of his napkin—once
again proposed. Italians speak in palinodes. To one
another and at double speed to a foreigner. A single case
in point . . .

Early in my expatriate life, I sat in the sweat- and
pee- and expensive-perfume-smelling first-class compartment of an early morning Milano-bound train. Alone
with a man, he having contributed more than I to the
expensive-perfume part of the carriage's atmosphere. Dark
tweeds, dark eyes; from Santa Lucia until moments before
our arrival at Centrale and in a voice more paternalistic
than lascivious, he'd proposed the ecstasies of my spending
the afternoon with him. Eloquently he proceeded with his
recital while I looked out the window. Every now and
then, though, I couldn't help turning a disdainful gaze at
him, at his absurdities. The only time I'd spoken was to a
conductor when, while the train was still waiting to depart
Venice, he'd entered to take tickets. Intermittently during
the journey I would leave the compartment, peruse the
cars for an alternate post. The few seats that remained
or became open promised even less serenity than my
own with the soft-spoken gallant. As the train lunged
into Milano Centrale I stood, gathered my things, wished

the fine-smelling dark tweeds a good day. Still sitting, he placed his hand lightly on my arm. Dark eyes laughing then, he told me, *I suppose you think I have been propositioning you. Ah,* cara straniera, *how you have misunderstood me. You may know the words,* poveretta, *but what are words without the legacy of a few thousand years of metaphorical implication?*

Spurned, he would not let me go without assuring me it was I who'd been. Spurned. A canny device used to brilliant ends in chess, in fencing, in any sort of war between foes or lovers or seat mates on a train. That Filippa sustained a point of view for half a morning and most of an afternoon—even if it was a point of view which I could not share—has refreshed me.

I shine my boots with a *calzonetto* but still they're scuffed and Tuscan earth clings to the Doc Martens' cleats. Olive oil on an already shredding dishcloth, I massage the time-softened leather, bang them against the side of the house to release the dried mud on the soles. Better. From my lean stash of clothes I choose a long skinny black skirt and over it layer an old Marithé black dress, tying its split skirt in a knot on one hip. Frozen in a half knee bend I braid my hair in front of the Campari Soda mirror, pin the thick coppery plaits just above my forehead. Won't Miss Antonia be surprised that a heathen American uses tortoiseshell pins just like hers. Opium. *Pronta.*

The main gate of Castelletto is 1.2 kilometres up a white gravel road from the place where the creek path ends. So says Biagio. Bluish clouds shroud half a May moon in the darkening sky as I start up the hill, a small wooden box of Montanucci chocolates in my purse. Fernando's gift sacrificed to my hostess.

I think of Biagio as I walk. As he does most afternoons, he came to tea today at five. A free-form ritual ours; if I've gone to the village at that hour or he finds himself still occupied, both know the other one will understand. Sometimes he brings Giorgia along. More usually, he comes alone. Today, post Filippa's—what did she call it?—*volubility*, I welcomed the salve of dear Biagio. As he does always, he announced himself in falsetto: '*Amore mio, sono io.*'

'*Vieni, vieni, sono qua.*'

Entering, he hangs on the doorknob his ancient grey *basco* with the torn black and white silk lining. Rubs his palms together as before a fire even when there is none. Or is it as before a thing which pleases him? So much pleases Biagio.

'*Come va?*' I ask, receiving, giving, a three-kiss kiss.

'*Magnificamente bene,*' he tells me.

'Darling Biagino, you seem *always* magnificently well?'

'I suppose I am. Maybe because of a certain thing my father told me when I was a boy. A man of very few words, one day when I was working beside him in the fields he stood up, looked down at me perched on my haunches, digging potatoes. He looked up at the sun, wiped his face with his sleeve. He said, "*La morte è più vicina della camicia, figlio mio.* Death is closer than your shirt, my boy." I had no idea what he meant, being eight or nine years old at the time. Maybe sixty years passed before I ever thought again about those words. It was one day when I was looking in the mirror and saw this old man looking back that I began to understand what my father had meant. *Death is closer than your shirt.* Since then, every morning when I reach for my shirt, before I put it on *io faccio le corna*—I make horns against death. So far it's worked damn well and I'll tell you that no matter what I'm doing or thinking or feeling, there's always some little sense of jubilance in having outwitted death one more time.'

I hold my fingers in the correct position: little one, pointer and thumb extended, the others folded back. I do it with both hands, extend both towards the stone floor. A general wish for good fortune.

'*Brava*,' he says, 'but tomorrow, remember about your shirt, will you?'

I make a tiny fuss about the tea, using things I've brought from home. A Staffordshire pot which he seems to love inordinately, running his work-thickened fingers over the blue and white pageant of crinolined and ringleted ladies taking tea under a willow by a stream. Two cups which almost match the pot in design if not colour. No sugar, no milk for us, only little saucers of jam or confiture—peach or fig from the markets or the rummed quince which Giorgia brings to me in litre-sized jars. I heat it almost to a liquid and we spoon it up like soup or stir it into our tea. Biagio likes this. He finishes, folds his napkin four times into a small triangle, places it on the tray for the next visit. Today I'd wanted to tell him about my time with Filippa but I didn't.

I reach the crest of the hill and there it is. Il Castelletto. Jesumaria, it's like a small village up here.

In riding boots and jeans, a white linen shirt billowing out from a thin, belted waist, an unbuttoned fawn-coloured suede vest, hair grizzled black and white and handsomely long, he steps from the penumbra of the grand, wide veranda into the yellow light of candle lanterns hung from its beams. In his arms he carries a mass of white lilac.

'*Buona sera, signora. Sono* Umberto. *Benvenuta a* Castelletto. *E' una serata splendida, no?* Good evening, I'm Umberto. Welcome to Castelletto. A splendid evening, wouldn't you say?' as he extends his elbow for me to shake, a gesture of greeting I thought exclusive to chefs with wet hands. I like this Umberto.

I make to open the door for him but Filippa is already there, standing three abreast with two of the others. Luce and Isotta. Luce being Filippa's sister—*perfect for the role of Castelletto emissary to the greater world*—Isotta, Filippa's younger daughter—*We did speak of rifts, yes? One might say that Isotta cultivates them.* I think I've got it straight.

One by one I take the extended hands, listen carefully to the self-introductions, try to fix names with faces, a not-so-simple task with this crowd of look-alikes. *Grazie, grazie*, I say to the *benvenuta* chorus as Antonia eases herself between them. Without a word she places her hand on the small of my back and, like a dancing teacher with a shrinking child, propels me over worn red tiles through a candlelit, tapestry-hung hall into a room as large as a cathedral.

'*Ecco*, behold,' she says. '*Si accomodi*. Be at home.'

Candlelight and firelight make an opaline mist of the air and one would be hard put to name the epoch of the endlessly long and enormously wide room. Low chestnut-beamed ceilings, red and yellow Turkey rugs flung over waxed tiles, the walls seem rouged like the ripe rose cheeks of a peach. Fat beeswax candles blaze like torches in black iron sconces set between long, leaded French windows open to the veranda and, beyond, to vines and olive trees and the twisted spires of the alps. Beeswax tapers in silver candelabra march along the centre of an unclothed refectory table, its ancient wood bleached from ancestral scrubbings. Fourteen armchairs in ivory canvas skirts are placed rather too widely along its monumental length. I can see now that the lilac are not white as I'd thought but of the palest yellow and whole limbs of them are twined among the arms and the feet of the candelabra. Lilac shudders in immense blue and white vases set on either side of an Empire sideboard, drips from shallow terracotta pots set beside yellow silk divans so that one brushes against it almost wherever one moves, sending the blossoms in small flurries onto the tiles and the rugs. In wide gilt cornices, *nature morte* from several epochs are hung one above another over an entire wall from just below eye level up to the beams. On every table and hearth shelf, and crowded inside glass-fronted cabinets, there are photographs in mostly tarnished silver frames. The only objects more plentiful than candles and photos are books. Piles teeter near every chair and floor-to-ceiling library stacks line the walls of an area at least twelve metres long. Burgundy velvet screens draped with long-fringed shawls divide the space but not so much into 'rooms' as into 'scenes'. At the far end begins the kitchen.

Candlelight surrenders to electricity via the fifteen-watt flame-shaped bulbs glimmering in wrought-iron chandeliers. It must always be dusk in Antonia's kitchen. Feather-plumped chairs and loveseats, a battered ebony baby grand, its lid unhinged, sit a few metres from work tables, two five-burner Bertazzoni, a white Aga. The four women are working at as many preparations, calling out to one another about progress, timing, about the events of their days. In between they sing *stornelli*—Tuscan folk-songs—with splendid Dantesque elocution, their glottal Cs almost Castilian. Antonia joins in. I wish I knew the words. Someone touches a switch and Vasco Rossi's haggard wail confides *un senso della vita*. This time I do know the words.

Heavy black cotton aprons over what look like 1940s vintage dresses—floral silks with gently padded shoulders, calf-length skirts—they seem affectionate kin, meddling in one another's work, singing at the top of rickety voices. Though Filippa is the elder sister by six or seven years, she appears far younger than Luce. Mary-Light, how I love her name. More chic, Luce, her hair is short, wisps of black curls falling over her cheeks. No chignon, no braids for her. Bronze shadows her lids, emboldens the hyacinthine blue of them . . . another kind of blue than Antonia's and Filippa's. Manicured nails, a Bulgari sapphire on her little finger, a matching bracelet hanging low on her wrist; I think what makes Luce seem older is how perfectly she's turned out. Isotta has quite the same features as the others but, less artfully arranged, they compose a less lovely face. Bosoms arched and firm above the bodices of their dresses, the same high, round derrières Italians call *alla Brasiliana*, what they all share is a nonchalant and therefore potent sexiness. All save Antonia. Spindly as a young tree, she sways, hums at the epicentre of the fray. I'm happy to be here.

'Have you ever tasted *carabaccia*?' Taking a breath from her singing, it's Luce who asks.

'Where would she have tasted *carabaccia*? Most Tuscans under the age of sixty—not to speak of foreigners—have never even heard of it.' It is Antonia who answers for me.

'Actually I do like it. Its history as much as the soup itself. Like so many other of her gifts, the French have gotten their mileage out of Caterina's little onion pap. Once they did away with the spices, that is. *Carabaccia* is a more beautiful name than *soupe à l'oignon*, though. Years ago at an antiques fair in Figline Valdarno I found four little boat-shaped baking dishes and I . . .' Thinking their collective silence is a sign that I've answered the question far too fully, I stop short. But the *truppa* is laughing and I wonder why.

'Ah, *mater mia*. Beware,' warns Luce. And I wonder about that, too.

For all the beauty of the place, all the treasures among which they live, there is nothing solemn or precious about their ways. Though Giorgia and Biagio help with the serving—as they help with so much of the running of things at Castelletto—they also sit and dine. They are decidedly family. This is not something I've seen, known about before.

Leaving more than half the table empty, Antonia pushes the chairs closer together, slides the plates and heavy silverware into new positions, Giorgia behind her, re-setting glasses. Antonia claps her hands. We sit. Biagio appears with two green-speckled jugs of cold white, then quickly with two more and everyone pours for someone else so that no one ever pours for herself. Himself.

Luce is at one end of the table, Antonia at the other. On one side there is Magdalena—Isotta's daughter, Antonia's great-granddaughter. The fresh eighteen-year-old Botticelli beauty of her helps one to see how the others must once have looked. She is partial to Antonia, coming to her often to embrace her, to smooth her hair, readjust a tortoiseshell pin. On Magdalena's right is Filippa, then Biagio, then Giorgia, then me, at Antonia's right. Across sits Giangiacomo—blond, gangly, blessed with a beautiful, timid smile—*fidanzato* to Magdalena. Guglielmo, Isotta and Umberto complete that side of the table.

As she cradles her chin in one hand, the other fiddling with her hair, I look at Miss Antonia up close for the first time. The colour of a pint of cream whipped with a tablespoon of vanilla, her skin. Milk stained with espresso. A long-limbed Juno posing as a Tuscan matron in a thin brown woollen dress and tiny-heeled black velvet sabots; if one would peruse the vast portfolio of the feminine genus bent on the archetypal goddess, one would stop at Antonia's portrait. Stop cold and close the book. I have yet to reconcile that she is eighty-three.

After the *brindisi*, when everyone rises, walks about to touch glasses with everyone else, Magdalena and Isotta begin passing trays of *bruschette* laid with roasted white asparagus. How delicate they are, plump, charred, leaving no wash of metal in the mouth, nothing to confuse the clean, acidic taste of Castelletto's *vernaccia*, the wine which is only one of Viola's masterworks, Antonia assures me. Giorgia is on her feet then, Isotta in pursuit, both clearing plates so that Luce and Filippa can set down small boat-shaped terracotta bowls fitted with lids.

Luce bends to smile at me as she places mine. 'Just like yours?'

When everyone is served and once again seated, Antonia gives the countdown and, operatically, lids are removed, the air suddenly fogged in clove and cinnamon steams. *Carabaccia*, of course. A fine spiced broth with onions caramelised to jam, the tiniest new peas were poached in it for a minute or two before white wine was splashed in for balance and intensity. The potion is lush. Tipping the big silver spoon of it into the mouth, breathing in the spice, one feels sorry for the French. Another configuration of the brigade clears the bowls, changes the silver.

It's Biagio alone who carries in the *arista*. Holding the white porcelain platter on upturned palms, he sets it down at Luce's place and she proceeds to carve. A white, fine-grained, boned loin of pork massaged with a paste of rosemary, young purple garlic, sea salt and good green oil, it was braised, *piano piano*, in *vernaccia* in the wood-fired oven on the veranda. The flesh falls to pieces under Luce's knife. As she carves, it's Filippa who lays each warmed plate with a purée of fresh fava beans, spooning pan juices over the velvety stuff, then more over the *arista*. Filippa and Magdalena pass clean plates, then set down two great white bowls of wild lettuces dressed only with oil and sea salt. How splendidly they work together, these daughters of Antonia, while she—Juno herself, smiling, laughing—leans towards me, almost complicitly, to say a few words under the din of the others.

Shallow blossom-edged soup plates hold the *fine pasto*, the end of the meal. Ewe's-milk ricotta made from last evening's milk—cooked and cooled—this morning's milk added, the mass cooked again. *Ri-cotta*. Re-cooked. How simple the Italian language can be. Embossed with the imprint of the old straw baskets in which it has drained all day, it is whiter than the porcelain white of the plates; the thick threads of chestnut honey drawn over it remind me of maple syrup drizzled over snow, and third graders in red rubber boots marching through winter woods. Pepper grinders are placed here and there on the table and passed along. Honey and pepper. A Renaissance duet of flavours reflecting life. Sweet and strong. *Dolceforte. Dolce salata.* Honey soothes. Pepper kicks. What would life be, one without the other?

'Oh yes, yes, I'm working very well,' I answer what I think must be Antonia's twice-asked question. She has just come back to her place after a turn around the table.

'*Bene. Mi fa piacere.* Good. That gives me pleasure.' She begins to say something else but I am distracted by Umberto's voice.

Up through the liveliness from his end of the table, I hear words and, intermittently, a phrase. It seems he speaks mostly to Isotta, to Luce, every now and then to Guglielmo, these three asking questions of him. *Ospitalità.* Hospitality. *Turismo.* Umberto says 'bed and breakfast' several times in English. So this is the rift about which Filippa spoke. Umberto, aided by Luce and once in a while by Isotta, speaks of a plan to transform abandoned properties into tourist lodgings, a country restaurant, a cooking school, a wellness centre. *Un complesso moderno,* he calls it, a modern complex. He is proud of the phrase, repeats it, tries it out in English. He runs out of fingers to count all the unused outbuildings waiting to be utilised: barns, stables, a watermill, a chapel, a cheese-making hut closed by the state fifteen years previously, six of the nine farmhouses once inhabited by de Gaspari farmers who, over time and the dissolution of the sharecropping system—the *mezzadria*—chose the convenience of modern apartment complexes in the nearby villages rather than the discomforts of tradition. He speaks of the dearth of rural yet elegant opportunities for tourists in this part of Tuscany. He refers at length to the successes of such places in the better known areas of Tuscany: the Val d'Orcia, the Chianti, the wine-producing areas around Montalcino and Montepulciano. No less charming, their own Tuscany, he says, no less rich their history and culture, and yet it is hardly known to the traveller, rarely touted in the travel journals . . .

'Alleluia for that,' Antonia says with just enough force to turn all attention back to her.

From her place furthest away down the table, Luce—cheeks wine-reddened, pushing damp ringlets off her forehead—looks at me, says, 'It's not as though we are all in agreement about the wisdom of this plan but, even if we were, none of it would ever come to be. Mother is a plutocrat.'

'And a xenophobe.' This is Isotta.

Are their thrusts at Antonia made of irony? Common dinner-table repartee? I think they are. Harmless, affectionate in their way.

'If wanting Tuscany to remain Tuscan means that I'm a xenophobe, then I am.' Antonia says this as though she's said it before.

A flight of laughter, a throwing up of hands. A refilling of glasses. Save those who are up and down with the last of the plates or setting out trays of *vin santo* and tins of *cantucci*, everyone is quiet as Umberto once again takes up his thesis. Everyone but Antonia.

Mid-phrase, she bursts in, 'Umberto, Umberto, since we have an American at table this evening and one who is involved, herself, with . . . what *is* it that you and your husband do? Something about *gite gastronomiche*, isn't it?' Antonia's voice has a tang, the promise of a burn. She baits rather than enquires. Has darling Juno turned hawk? And who was it to whom Luce said, *Beware*?

'Why don't you tell us about what you do?' she invites me.

Once again the room quietens and I long for Vasco Rossi. I peruse the table, scouting for allies. I turn to Antonia and say, '*Gite gastronomiche* compose only a small part of what I do, *signora*. Mostly what I do is hunt down the past. I stalk the storytellers, the country people, the ones who still live *come una volta*. I spur them on, the last ones who know how it *was*. And how it *tasted*. I want to be there when they cook, when they celebrate. I want to listen to them and I want to save what I hear.'

'And who are *you* to *want* all of that?'

There is a shuffling of feet. Quietly but not so that we don't hear her, Luce says, as though an unfed dog was loosed, '*E scatenata*. She's unchained.'

Once again, I look at Antonia. 'Not much of anyone, *signora*. Not much of anyone at all. I ask questions. You might find it surprising how many people *desire* to talk. How naturally they do it.'

'How quaint. You want to save *once upon a time* . . . And so the storytellers, what makes you think you understand what they say? I don't mean understand their language—I suppose you can do that well enough. But do you think you *comprehend* what they say?'

I think of the man on the train to Milano. *What are words without the legacy of a few thousand years of metaphorical implication?* 'Mostly I think I do. As much as anyone *comprehends* another. Language is the least essential part of empathy.'

Through eyes nearly closed I try to push Antonia out of my sight, send her further away than the six centimetres which separate us. I crush a *cantuccio* to crumbs in the fist of one hand, try to get my wineglass to my lips with the other. Breath comes in short stabs.

'Nonna, please.' It's Isotta who speaks. Some of the others mumble accord.

'Mother, *ti prego*.' This is Luce.

'*Sono mortificata*.' Now it's Filippa.

More shuffling, the pushing back of chairs. I try for my wineglass again and this time I can hold it. Sip from it. Guglielmo comes to Antonia, asks her if she wouldn't like to walk a bit with him and Isotta. She wouldn't, thank you. His cheeks red as mine feel, Giangiacomo shambles through the confusion and down to me, tells me how lovely it was to meet me. I stand to hug him, this boy I'd never seen before two hours ago, this gentleman-child who has himself likely been suppertime prey here in the yellow-rose lustre of Antonia's little castle.

Why am I still here? Why am I talking, smiling with everyone who passes by, as though the evening has been a bliss? *Buonanotte, certo, certo, ci sentiamo.*

Having wished Antonia a good night, kissed her hand, now Umberto turns to me, raises my hand to his lips, pulls me away from the table. 'Let me tell you a secret.'

'Is it that she does this only to people she likes?'

'Brilliant.'

'Why did you leave America for Italy?'

Talons retracted, Antonia has surrendered inquisition for interview. Or so it seems. The others dispersed, Filippa, Luce, Antonia and I have moved to sit by the hearth closest to the kitchen. Luce has brought in wood from the veranda, laid a fine fire. Someone brought in coffee. A few minutes earlier when I'd begun saying my good evenings, aching for a cleansing run all the way back down the white road to Biagino's lodge, it was Luce who asked me to stay.

If you leave now—if you leave without Mother's having some chance to redeem herself . . . You see, it's not you she attacked. You understand that, I know you do. She named you the evening's scapegoat, a pleasure many others have had before you. If you leave now . . . Please don't go. Not yet.

Luce and Filippa and a cat called Filoush share a sofa in front of the fire. Antonia and I sit across from each other in two wine-red damask chairs. The right positioning for a stand-off. With a goddess? With a hawk? Luce's words have put me almost at ease. I want to listen more than I want to be understood. I learn more by trying to understand than by trying to be understood. Just as I felt with Filippa up in the woods this afternoon, I want to leave and I want to stay. Antonia can't hurt me. No one can.

On the battered baby grand nearby Isotta plays badly in a heartfelt way and we four sit smoking Gitanes without filters, stirring cognac into gold-rimmed, footed porcelain cups of *caffè* thick and black as a Turk's. We cross our legs, uncross them.

'I didn't leave America for Italy,' I tell Antonia. 'I left America for a man. If he'd been an Argentine, it's in Buenos Aires where I might be this evening.'

'You'll pardon me if I don't ask you to pursue that . . . I fear my candid response to the story of a woman—of a certain age—leaving whatever life she may have had in her native country to chase a man . . . well . . .'

'Hardly a chase, *signora*. Not a chase.'

Standing to meddle a poker in the fire, Antonia is quiet. Agile diplomats calming their mother's wake, Luce and then Filippa ask about Fernando, how we met. I answer in a fashion, all the while looking at Antonia, wondering what hurts her so.

Turning from the fire, Antonia says, 'Political refugees, religious ones, those who flee to survive, these I understand. But if one is born, grows up in a place, the place where one's history is, and then one packs up, runs away . . . what is it? To find one's self? To lose one's self? It seems a skittish move. What is the essential desire of the expatriate? To begin again? Another chance? I often think it's something like divorce. One leaves a person and, with an often whiplash speed, one finds another person, sets the process in motion all over again, the process and its motion following familiar lines. It must be the same with leaving one country for another. What didn't seem right or good in one country may swiftly begin to seem not *right*, not *good* in another. All this motion, this changing partners, changing cultures . . . it's a lack of discipline. If only people would understand that what needs to be changed is themselves.'

I hear Emily saying, *So I'll try a different dream, the one where I come to live in Italy. After all, living here, just going out to buy a sack of tomatoes becomes a foray into another world . . . and then I'd find the right man and . . .*

Luce is asking Antonia, 'What has such a decision to do with discipline, Mother? Can't you accept that one might choose to live in Italy because one is happier here?'

'Because one is happier or because one *imagines* one will be happier? As though joy grew like a wild grass in Tuscany. A fool's notion. There isn't any *place* in the world that can transform an unhappy soul. No light, no air, no sea, no meadow or mountain or charming little village. Certainly no *man*. Not even if an unhappy person sets up among those who *are* content, not even that will help for very long. In fact, wandering among the peaceful is perilous. It illuminates one's own emptiness. There are no miracles to be had from geography.'

'I agree, *signora*, no miracles to be had from geography.' My instinct is to pacify her. To assuage her thirst for battle by refusing to fight.

Still standing, Antonia turns back to the fire. Arms resting on her hips, hands to the warmth, she wants to know, 'Do you think Italy has not enough chroniclers and storytellers and cultural interpreters of its own? Do you think there is a need for strangers to tell us about ourselves?'

'I don't write the stories for you, *signora*. Not for Italians. For the others. I write them for the *outsiders*. The ones like me. The ones who long to wander over the old stones, watch the light. Those who, even for a while, want to *be* in the Italy they dream of.'

'I can hardly believe the greater world needs one more book to feed its appetite for Italy. I understand you wrote a book about Venice. When I heard that, well, it made me laugh. Yours must have been the fifty thousandth book written about that filthy, swamp-smelling Byzantine hole and I can't imagine a reader left on earth who'd pay a price for it.'

'A few were willing,' I tell her.

Luce laughs. Antonia asks her, *Why is that so humorous?*, but she doesn't answer.

'What was left to write about Venice?' she persists. 'Surely not the Venetians, since there are no more. Only vulgar hordes of tourists. But, unlike the would-be Venetians who have set up to stay, at least the tourists go away. So many of the *palazzi* on the canal have been taken over by strangers that all one hears are the American twang and the nasty haut-British garble. We shan't even speak of the others. They all emigrate from the same Hell, though. They emigrate from Cash. Sometimes from Credit. Sometimes even from Debt. They're generally an avaricious lot, lusting after something the neighbours back home in Hell don't have yet. They walk heavily over the old city's heart. And the culture sinks faster than the stones. How wise of you to have escaped.'

'I would have stayed forever, *signora*. It was my husband who wanted to leave Venice.'

'You *enjoyed* living in Venice?'

'Immensely.'

'You hardly paint an attractive self-portrait. Certainly not the one the world has come to believe as typical of a twenty-first-century American woman. You leave your life to join his, you admit an *immense* pleasure in the new place and then, *oopla*, you pack up and follow him again . . .'

'Something like that, *signora*.' Even as I answer Antonia, it is with a weak will to convince her. Whether she approves, damns, it doesn't matter. Despite the pompous delivery, some of her observations hit bullseye. Close to bullseye. As for the rest, maybe I'll learn something if I stay quiet.

My docility infuriates her. She turns and pokes again in the fire, a surgeon palming a point of entry for her knife. 'What else have you written?'

'A book about Tuscany. About the two years we lived in San Casciano dei Bagni.'

'Toscana? Also Tuscany? Well, I'm content to hear that, since it must mean you're already on to other regions. What's next for you? Calabria, *forse*? *Oppure* Sardegna? Anything would be better than those *traipsing through the hilltowns* books promising a troupe of dancing peasants and true love with a broken-down count to . . . I can hardly imagine the number of ageing, fading women in America and England—and who knows where else—who consider smothering their snoring, pot-bellied husbands with a pillow so they can run off to Italy to begin again.'

She pauses, awaiting my response but, as though I haven't heard her or, better, that she has spoken to no effect, I sit quietly. Benignly. My defence is to treat Antonia as a naughty child. To let her have her way until, exhausted by her own perversity, she will fall fast asleep where she sits.

Still she strikes another time. 'And then for the poor wretches who are condemned to stay where they are, there's

Tuscan-style this and Tuscan-style that . . . *Tuscan* having become the ornamental adjective of choice for uninformed journalists all over the world. I saw a preposterous display in a magazine on an aeroplane: *Tuscan Farmhouses in Santa Fe.* As though primping up a space with plastic beams and factory tiles, a pot of rosemary and a few chestnuts thrown down on a table could make it Tuscan. A spoiled child's caprice. Always wanting more, always wanting different. Always wanting what the others have. I suppose you've put your signature on a line of Tuscan pillows or some such, have you?'

'I have not.'

'Good. Now tell me about your fairytales.'

'Not fairytales. Not fairytales at all. I tell the stories that people tell to me. Or I tell stories about what happened to me. What happened to people I know.'

'I still can't grasp the draw of a memoir written by, you'll pardon me, an *unknown*. Who are you and what have you done and who are your friends and what have *they* done that any of your lives would interest others?'

'Mother, I beg you . . .' With her eyes, Luce beseeches Filippa for aid but Filippa is occupied with smashing the tip of a half-smoked Gitane into a silver ashtray, then lighting another one.

'Assuming you write in English, have your books been translated into other languages?' Antonia asks.

'Yes. Yes, fourteen or fifteen. Perhaps more.'

'Is German one of the languages?'

'Yes. Yes, it is.'

'And these books that you write about yourself and your friends, they inspire others to do what you did, yes? Make people want to come to live here, yes?'

'It's not my intention to encourage or convince. How people respond to what I write belongs to them.'

'Yes, yes, of course. That belongs to them.' Antonia says this last very quietly. A whisper. Perhaps the naughty child tires at last.

'Would you like to go upstairs now, Mother?' Luce asks her. 'Filippa and I will walk down to the lodge with Marlena and . . .'

But Antonia is stabbing fresh ground. 'Tell us about your work with tourists.'

'Fernando and I host very small groups of English-speaking travellers who are interested in knowing about regional food and wine, culinary history, that sort of thing.

Only several weeks a year, mostly during the *vendemmia* and the *raccolta*.'

'Another expatriate cooking school; so that's what you do. I hadn't realised it was that.'

'It's not. Not a *cooking school* at all. Sometimes I offer demonstrations of a dish or two but mostly we're out in the fields, among the vines, in the orchards, visiting the artisans, dining with families, sometimes in typical restaurants . . . It's really quite—'

'And how did you come to be the expert . . . or is expertise conferred with one's *carta d'identità*? An expatriate privilege? You know a little and they know nothing and so, somewhat like the professor who reads the text he will teach that day while breakfasting, you're half a pace ahead. Is that it?'

'Mother, please.' Filippa is tamping out another unsmoked cigarette, lighting the next.

'*Expertise* is not what I propose,' I say. 'Our offer is simple: the chance for a traveller to walk about with someone who lives and works and cooks and eats and drinks in Italy and who can tell them about all of that in their own language.'

'Wouldn't it be more authentic if an Italian did what you do? If a local person escorted strangers through his everyday life? There *are* Italians who speak English.'

'Yes. It might be. Depending on what sort of Italian was doing the hosting. It's mostly readers of my books who come to be with us. The tours become an extension of the books. Guests want to see the places I write about. They want to *be* where we are. I guess they want also to *feel* what I feel. They want to step through a magic door. Actually, sometimes they don't work out very well, the tours. I feel sad when a guest goes away wishing he'd spent his money in some other way, even though I know that sort of guest would go away wishing he'd spent his money in some other way no matter where he went. A while ago I laughed to myself a bit in recognition when you said one shouldn't expect *miracles of geography*. I'd add: nor of authors. Of course, there are tours when things work so beautifully that no one wants the time to end.'

'And when that happens, a session with an estate agent follows—is that it?'

'It hasn't been but I suppose it could be. Italy does have a rather long and constant history of embracing expatriates. I doubt my humble activities are having much of an effect on the number of—'

'Mother is against any active seduction of foreigners, of the ones looking to set up here. Those who would acquire land. Especially land. Abandoned houses.' Luce looks at Antonia as she speaks to me.

'I find it disquieting,' Antonia says, 'to walk on the corso in Pienza on a Sunday afternoon with my cousins and their neighbours and hear not a word of Italian spoken save by the merchants along the way or *i branchi di vecchietti*, the groups of old men who gather in the bars after their naps. It's all German, Dutch, English, English, English. And these are not passers-by but a new species of locals.'

'I should think you'd be more disquieted by the folks of Pienza themselves. The ones who, for whatever reasons, have chosen to sell out. Foreigners can't buy what's not for sale.'

Antonia tinkers with her cup, spoons up the dregs, pours a few drops of cognac into the empty cup, sips it. 'Yes. Yes. *Divindenaro* rules. Divine *gelt*. Money. Even in Pienza. Pocketsful of gold, heritage cast off, people go to live in cement boxes down in the valleys, settle themselves in front of the television, wait out whatever time is left . . .'

'There's no dearth of the younger who yearn to sell off their inheritances so they can live a life different from the one their parents lived. All this coming and going and trading places in the world, the search for something new . . . it's the way it's been always . . .'

'Are you about to give me a history lesson? Will you begin with the Phoenicians? The Etruscans? Will you tell me that twelve thousand years before Christ, invaders were roaming over the peninsula? Most of them liking what they saw, some of them desiring to stay? Don't trouble yourself. Hardly a salve, all that. What does help is to remember that there are still a few Tuscans who hold tight to their connection with the past. The far past, the tribal past. I think that's one of the things the rest of the world wants from us, that feeling of belonging. They want to inhabit our skins. They want to *be* us. Setting up here with shiny new garden tools and boxes full of cookbooks, sprawling in the pool built over the bones of twenty generations of farmers who bathed in a creek or a river or, more likely, not at all. Well, they can sprawl all they want, play *living in Italy* till they croak, but never will they belong. *Connection* is not for sale, not transferable. It comes only through the blood.'

'You make a grave error, *signora*, thinking it's trouble-some to a person who comes to live here from somewhere else to accept that he does not *belong*. It's true that the illumination smarts a bit at first but it's easily enough consoled by clinging to other expatriates. By living in *colonies*. Just as Filippa suggested to me earlier.'

'Touché.' It's Filippa who says this, very quietly. She proceeds then, 'Mother, Marlena has heard all of this . . .'

Antonia ignores her. 'I have nothing against foreigners as long as they're content to visit, even to stay a while. To come back. But not to set up. I'm quite generous on that point even though most of them simply don't know how to behave. Or even know where they are. I've heard more than one of them asking some fool with a red umbrella *Are we in Tuscany yet?*, as they're wandering the streets of Pienza or Massa or Firenze. Not the ghost of an idea where they are, and nor do most of them care as long as they can drink and eat and buy shoes. Despicably loud and parading about in cyclist's pants, you can hardly tell the men from the women, all of them with cropped white hair and gym shoes and bulging veins and those ugly purses strapped around fat middles. A vulgar sight.'

Luce says, 'Mother doesn't like the way we dress either, thinks women over the age of forty should wear tea dresses after six and fix their long thick curly hair in a chignon . . .' She runs her fingers through her short hair and, with her palms, presses ringlets first on one cheek, then the other.

I ask Antonia, 'What do you think Italians do when they travel? Do you think they don't move in packs and dress badly and shout in the streets?'

'Of course they do. But that's not my concern. Besides, they go away again. They don't haunt real estate agents and covet a house in Vermont. Or a flat under the pyramids. They come back home.'

'Droves of them have emigrated to all parts of the world.'

'I'm not speaking of emigration. For purposes of survival, of asylum. We've been through that argument.' She stays quiet, gathering strength. 'As I said, I admire travellers. They are altogether different from tourists. People who want to see the world, to walk in the past. What is it, Luce? Is it eighty-five percent of the world's artistic patrimony that sits in Italy?'

'Seventy-five of the eighty-five being in Roma, Mother. Relatively little of it in Toscana.'

'Then why does everyone want to come here? Right here. Exactly here.'

'They don't. Just as Umberto says, they want *that* Tuscany. The Goths are not making their way up the mountain, Mother,' Luce tells her.

Antonia looks at Luce and smiles. She laughs a tinkly faraway laugh, says, 'But they did once. And it's for certain of my memories of their "sojourn" here in these mountains that I flinch at the prospect of Germans acquiring land, a house here in the very place where, not so many years ago, their fathers, grandfathers murdered and . . .' More quietly she says, 'There is a certain profanity in their—'

'The Germans who might want to own land and a home in Tuscany now had nothing to do with those events. Your arguments are puerile, Mother. Both puerile and pompous. You have grown ridiculous in your dotage,' Luce tells her.

'Have I? Perhaps. Better to let the past lie, is that it? For longer than sixty years and with all my heart, I tried to reach that state of grace, assuring myself, *No use trying to get at the juices of the past, because there aren't any. All dried up, all dust. What can be served by kneeling before the past or hiding behind it?* Well, it worked. It worked somewhat and for a while. It helped that someone was always hungry or hurt or dying or getting born and something always wanted cooking or planting or harvesting or washing or patching. Distractions which have grown powerless by now. I think what *was* puerile of me was to believe I could turn the other cheek. To hell with the other cheek.'

Filippa rises, goes to stand behind her mother's chair, reaches down to caress her shoulders, bends to press her lips to Antonia's grey-brown head. 'Mamma.'

'I thought I had no choice. I did, though. I still do. I think we almost always do.'

'Mamma, it's late and I think you—as well as I, this afternoon . . . well, Marlena has had enough initiation into the life and times of Antonia Ducchi de Gaspari and her spawn,' Filippa says.

Antonia leans her head back to look up at Filippa. Smiles. Both are weeping.

Luce says to me, 'I shall not apologise for this mildly grotesque little spectacle. I'm sorry I asked you to stay. Mother's parlour manners are always somewhat piquant but . . .'

I look at Luce, shake my head, mumble, 'Don't worry . . . it's okay . . .'

Luce continues, 'Earlier, Isotta called Mother a xenophobe. It's not true, Marlena. Mother's phobia, her antipathy—no, her *odium*—is reserved for Germans. Any German. All Germans.' Though Antonia begins to speak, Luce keeps her gaze on me.

'I own that. I own that. But there are exceptions, *piccola* Luce.' Antonia rests her head against the high red chair. Her gaze upward, open hands smoothing the folds of her dress. 'The impulse to ruthlessness may be the single trait humans, all humans, share. I propose that the intensity of the impulse is more malignant in the Hun. The bastard Hun. And don't any one of you bother with a litany of the fiendish acts perpetrated by every race on earth. I know about them. I do not discount them. But the particular breed of fiendishness that was perpetrated here, right here in the room where we now sit with our cups and our fire . . .'

An arm about my shoulders, it is Filippa who urges me out of the *salone* through one of the doors to the veranda, walks with me down the white gravel road, neither of us speaking of the evening, the afternoon, of Antonia, of Luce. Of the Goths who once climbed the mountains or of the ones who someday might. When I stop for a moment, tell her I'd like to walk the rest of the way alone, she nods, says, 'We've made a mess of it, haven't we, Mamma and Luce and I?'

'If you mean, *for me*, then no. Not for me. Not for me at all.'

I stop by the creek to take a bottle of icy water from the little stone chamber which Biagio has built for me against the verge. I don't switch on Venus but feel about for the matches on the table and light a candle, open the water and drink it, gulp it, let it dribble onto my chin and my chest as though the fine prickly stuff was a potion that would bring me back through the looking glass. But it doesn't.

I undress, let my things lie where they fall, step into my nightdress, carry the candle to the nightstand, climb up onto the princess bed. I note that it's the first time I have felt truly alone here in the old stone house in the woods.

What is it about Antonia? This German obsession. Its proportions are ferocious. To rave that since my books are translated into German, I am encouraging Germans to settle in Tuscany?

Xenophobia, plutocracy, swimming pools built over the bones of ten generations of Tuscan farmers, oil barons, Goths climbing the mountains, the Occupation, bed-and-breakfast lodges, the other Tuscany, the next Tuscany, carabaccia, *ruthlessness, odium. Antonia Ducchi de Gaspari and her spawn. Vasco Rossi. Jesumaria.*

I know sleep won't come tonight and so I get up, pull on my boots since I can't find my slippers, go to light a fire even though it's not so cold in the lodge. I'm hungry. There's nothing but wine and an onion in the little fridge. And a bit of pasta left from yesterday's lunch, *penne rigate*—cooked, undressed. I remember the two eggs which Giorgia leaves every morning in the wire basket hanging by the side door. I light a burner on the stove, slam Biagio's heavy iron skillet down on it, pour in a good amount of oil. When it's hot I add the cooked pasta, roll it about with a wooden spoon and leave it to crisp while I slice the onion very thinly, then into the pan. I rub sea salt over the mass, break a few fennel seeds in the mortar and add them as well. I pluck a small *peperoncino* from the sheaf of them which is my inside door decoration, rub it between my palms into the pan. When the pasta is golden, the onions soft, the perfume delicious, I beat the eggs, spread them evenly over the pasta. I leave it then, go to pour what's left of a bottle of *vermentino* into the flute reserved for Fernando's prosecco. The occasion merits all the beauty I can scrape together. I reverse the frittata onto a pot lid, slide it back into the pan, let it cook another minute or two while I fill the green pitcher with red from the barrel. I cut the frittata in two, set myself up by the fire. I eat slowly, concentrate on every mouthful. I drink deeply of the wine. All the while I try to take in not so much what Antonia said as what she did not say. Her lacunae. That's where her story is. In the fragments of the fresco she left unpainted. I understand I played understudy to Antonia's demons, a role I've been cast in before, one for which I must surely have some talent. One bent on assault is wont to confound the other's passivity, mistake it for weakness, but Antonia didn't do that with me. I wouldn't flinch and she liked that. Takes one to know one.

I open the spigot and let more of Biagio's red splash into the green pitcher. Over and over again I hear Luce saying, *Mother's phobia, her antipathy—no, her odium—is reserved for Germans. Any German. All Germans.*

I own that. I own that, piccola *Luce. But there are exceptions.*

I get up to fetch the other half of the frittata.

CHAPTER V

The knock is decidedly not Biagino's. Nor Giorgia's. Besides, it's not yet dawn. My body towel-wrapped, my head half braided, I shout, '*Arrivo, arrivo.*'

Dropping the towel, stepping back into my nightdress, I pull aside the bathroom curtain to find her sitting at the table.

'The high meadow was full of them this morning.' She pulls a dirt-crusted wild onion out of a canvas sack which spills over with them. 'They'd make a fine *carabaccia*, don't you think?'

I stand there looking from the onions to her face, back to the onions. 'Can't say until I taste one.'

Neither of us makes a move or a sound, as though we're thinking hard on something. Deciding something. Though surely not about the onions. Then Antonia laughs. She laughs harder. Unslept, undressed, and understanding the onions are her olive branch, I laugh with her.

'I'll just wait while you finish your toilette. I have espresso in a thermos. I'll take you to where the onions are,' she says, the wonder in her eyes worthy of a promise to show me a herd of white unicorns. 'I trust you don't take sugar.'

'No sugar,' I tell her as I gather up yesterday's clothes. A quick riffle through my bag of lingerie and socks. As I retreat behind the green curtain, she's sweeping the hearth. I hear her piling wood. She sings. I must be taking too long because she goes outdoors then, sweeps the stones, opens and closes the shutters.

'*Festina lente*,' she shouts from outside. 'Make haste slowly. The light won't wait, you know.'

It's not three minutes later that I'm zipping up my jacket, tying my bootlaces, racing out the open door, but she's gone. I circle the lodge, walk a bit along the creek path, sit near the water to watch the darkness shatter and break into lilac dust. *She's a strange one.*

'Any moment now,' she says from somewhere behind me.

'*Signora?*' I turn around and can barely make out the figure of her up above, sitting on one of the stone benches where Filippa and I were yesterday.

'Stay where you are,' she warns, as a great rubescent flash stains the sky in all the reds of the world.

A moment later, I make my way up to her. She hands me a little glass cup of espresso, pats the place next to her. I prefer to stand, I say. She lifts skinny-fingered hands to snatch a tortoiseshell pin from the unkempt chignon of her grey-brown curls, pushes a wind-ruffled strand away from her eyes. Shards of silver swimming in ice blue. She wears a belt of mended black leather over what must be her daytime brown dress, as opposed to the somewhat finer one she wore last evening. In the small pockets which hang from the belt there are scissors, a spade, a knife. Curious, her jewels. On the stone seat, fussing with her hair, she seems grown up from the scene, an indigenous flower. This is her place. She belongs to it as it does to her. She laughs then, perhaps for nothing less than the joy of it, her cheeks colouring not red but tawny, like a sunburnt child's.

'Shall we walk for a while?' she invites.

Single file up a path into a chestnut wood where I've never been, she leads the way, sets the pace, talks over her shoulder. 'I *am* sorry, you know. But not for my general sentiments regarding interlopers.'

'No. I wouldn't think so.'

'But I was harsh with you—*arrogant*, as Filippa said later. I prefer arrogance to puerility, though.'

'I felt a whack on the nape of the neck only once.'

'When?'

'Maybe we could talk about that another time.'

'Why did you come with me this morning?'

'Not sure. Maybe because I'm wondering what it could be that hurt you so? I mean about the Germans. It's not as though I'm asking for an answer.'

'Good. Because there's none coming.'

The wood opens upon a high plateau. A room in the sky. Mists hang still in the tender light and a low-slung wind ripples the grasses, flutters the hem of Antonia's dress. A pastoral goddess bending to a patch of tiny-leafed *rucola*, she is at work with a small green spade.

'Sprouted up overnight, look at it all. And if the rain doesn't fall too hard, there'll be more tomorrow. May's *rucola* is sharp as mustard.' She stops her work to pull a knife from her belt, holds it out to me.

'I've got my own.'

'*Brava*. As you'll see, there's more than *rucola* here. Separate the weeds to eat raw from the ones to cook. You know the difference, I imagine.'

'I do in Umbrian meadows.'

She laughs, stops and looks up at me. 'Two centimetres of root, no more or—'

'They won't grow again. Less than that and all that's good in them is left behind. I've had a good teacher.'

Dandelions, wild chicory, wild carrot, wild parsnip, goat's beard, hawkweed, more *rucola*, more wild onions; I heave the bounty into two piles: those to eat raw, those to boil then fry in oil with *peperoncini* and fat cloves of garlic.

'Every chance you get, pass on what you know. About weeds—especially about weeds. Books can't teach the way a person can. Around here it was always mother to child, mostly mother to daughter. Like a doe teaching her fawn. What to eat, what to leave. Did you run away from home? Is that why you're here?' She's come closer to where I'm digging, wrapping lengths of thick weed around my piles, adding them to her sack.

I look up at her. 'No. Nothing like that.'

'What's it like being married to a Byzantine? Giorgia says he's *stupendo*. Marvellous.'

'She'd be right. Biagino offered me the lodge so that I could—'

'I know all about the *premise* of why you're here.'

'I think the *premise* is all there was to the decision. I need to work.'

'I can understand that. The *nostrum* of work. The urgency of it.'

'Deadlines.'

'Yes. The deadlines. In my case, deadlines are imposed by the sun and at what moment it will rise. I have a great job, this gathering weeds. And making supper.'

'Mine's a good job, too.'

'I imagine it is. Almost any job one can do alone is a good job. People who work alone know the beauty of solitude. The perhaps greater beauty of loneliness. But you haven't had much opportunity to arrive at that exalted state since you've been here, have you? He's come to visit, what, ten times in five weeks? Your Byzantine.'

'No. Just once a week. Friday afternoons. He stays until Monday morning.'

'I'd say if you didn't run away it's only because he cut you off at the pass.'

'Maybe it was a kind of running away. But with a tether.'

'The way children run away.'

'Something like that. Like running away to the back garden. With Fernando as my tether. But it wasn't *away* from him that I ran but *towards* him. After two years of drama around the work on our apartment, I thought our longed-for settling-in would mark another beginning. And for me, it might have. But for Fernando it turned out to be an ending. A dead stop. With the workmen gone, he no longer had a job. No one left to inspect and cajole and direct. I had my work but he had none. A reversal of our earlier situation: when I moved to Venice, he had his work and I had a fresh white page on which to reinvent myself . . . no language, no job, no house, no kith, no friends. Like a child, I trusted—myself, him, the Fates—and struck out to find my way. But when it happened to him, he withdrew. Even though it was his own fresh white page which he'd insisted he wanted, when he had it, it frightened him. I think that's what happened.

And so it followed naturally that, since I *did* have work, he would come to resent the time that it and I stole from him. What I wanted was for him to take that "fresh white page" and run with it. Explore, pursue one thing then another until he found what pleased him, intrigued him. After spending most of his adult life working at a job which was imposed on him, I thought—and he did, too—the liberty of the white page would excite him. That's what *I* wanted for him but, as it turned out, that's not at all what he wanted for himself. His white page was quickly stuffed away because what he wanted was to play house, he wanted more of our little journeys here and there over every corner of the peninsula. He wanted to be together. He wanted us to have the *same* white page. And so finding the peace in which to work, well, it became difficult. That's about where we were when Biagio took over.'

'And now? Where are you now?'

'Where we were five weeks ago, save that I'm in a better place with my work. And I think that Fernando is in a better place with his patience, his understanding about my writing life. Also I think each of us has regained our humility. A perilous business, I think, to move about without it. Fernando's high horse may have run away but I gave my own a farewell pat. Mine's gone, too.'

'Then it served. *Lascialo da solo*. To leave him by himself for a while. To give him less time than he wants, less of *you* than he wants. But the rub is that you also have less of him than you want. I can see that.'

'Am I so limpid as that?'

'In this case. But I would think not often.'

Even as I speak to her about myself, about him, I regret it. I stop a moment, bend down to tie my perfectly tied boots. She walks on ahead.

'I'd rather we talked about you. Actually, I'd rather that you talk and I listen,' I tell her when I catch up.

We'd stopped digging and cutting a while ago, left behind Antonia's sack and the portion of my piles that wouldn't fit in it, and now we're just meandering over the field, she stopping now and then to point out one thing or another. To stuff her pockets with wild mint.

'Beware asking me to talk. If you think Filippa wore out your ears yesterday, understand that her stamina pales next to mine.'

'I'll risk it.'

'I may, too. Risk it. Someday. But for now, well, let's see . . . I will tell you that I no sooner lay my head down to sleep before I start longing for the morning. I often think what a waste of time the night can be and wish that soon after it set, the sun would rise again. Before it does, I do. I wash my face and brush my teeth, step into my dress, my boots, fasten the tools around my waist, take the thermos Luce leaves in the kitchen for me, grab my sack. Traipsing down the oak walk while the air is still bluish, the sea thumping below, the bells droning out the call to matins, my heart ticking nicely in my chest, I find it all thrilling in its way. Going to see what's thrust into bud, poked up from the earth, turned yellow, turned green, turned sweet and ripe, I bend and sniff and touch, start digging and snipping and filling my sack. There's always something; the earth is loyal. It asks less than people do. Ah, what to do with a windfall of wild *rucola*? A thought like that can shape a day. Maybe as good a day as any day in a life.'

'But this isn't where you grew up. I mean, this isn't where you were born. I recall Biagio saying that you're from . . .'

'No, this is not where I was born. I came to live at Castelletto when I married. I was almost eighteen. These

fields and meadows and woods, as far as you can see and
further yet, became my legal fiefdom thirty years ago but
still it's not *my* land as much as the little farm where I was
born. I go back there as often as I can. To walk about, to
visit with the family who's been living there and working
the land since—well, since a long time ago. *I* Gozzoli.
Eraldo Gozzoli. He's long gone but his sons and their
sons—sixty years or so of Gozzoli men and their wives
and children—are taking care of things. Now it's two of
Eraldo's grandsons and their wives and a granddaughter
and her husband and their children who live together in
that old *casolare*. There's a once-upon-a-time tribe for you.
Self-sustaining, or nearly so, and thick as thieves. One
for all, all for one, that sort of family. And not a single
one of them with a bed-and-breakfast fantasy. We'll go
together one day if you wish. Not the sort of place *Santa
Fe Living* would choose to photograph, mind you.'

Also Miss Antonia is sharp as May *rucola*. 'So what
will you do with it? The *rucola*,' I ask.

'Very little. Rinse and dry it, leave it in a damp towel
in a cool place until lunch. Dress it with sea salt and
oil. I'll pound what's left with a few walnuts and drops
of oil, add some pecorino to make a paste—not thick,

not thin—spread it on roasted bread to begin tonight's supper. However many of the blue-eyed, high-bottomed, high-strung hellions are in-house at six thirty, they gather in the kitchen to cook. You'd be welcome.'

'Not quite ready for a reprise of . . .'

'Still feeling a sting, are you?'

'Maybe a little. But that's not the only reason I won't come.'

'*Come volete*. As you wish. Time for a rest, wouldn't you say?'

No trees to lean against, no smooth stone benches, we sit among the weeds now, our legs out straight—old, half-broken dolls lolling on the nursery floor. We sip the last of the espresso.

Words flitting, unsaid, about her lips and eyes, Antonia looks at me, looks away. She asks, 'Have you ever been hungry? Not a bit late to supper but *hungry*?' Less than to me, she addresses some larger audience gathered in her mind's eye. 'Never lived through a war, either, have you? Or worked fifteen hours a day in the fields under the sun, under the flaying sun with a heel of bread to keep you upright, maybe a crumble of cheese and a fistful of grasses like these.' She rakes a hand through the weeds, pulls up a clump by its roots. 'Never squatted under a tree to deliver a baby, cut its cord with your pocket knife, sucked the phlegm from its nose and mouth, swaddled it, tied it to your chest and gone back to digging potatoes. Nor did your father ever invite his *padrone* to ease himself down from his horse of an evening and onto your nubile loins? A little gift, man to man . . . ? No, none of that.'

She looks at me and I can't tell if the desired result from her soliloquy is shock or sympathy. I feel neither. 'Did any of those things happen to you?' I ask her.

'Not to me. But all of that was everyday life around here not so long ago.'

'And with a few variables in the text, you could be describing how women have lived—still live—in any country on the planet. The have-nots, the abused, the vanquished: despair has not been exclusive to Italy. And, as the world is now, Italy counts fewer humiliations than—'

'I asked you last evening not to bother with a litany of what's evil in the world. It's these cinematic images— licence, heat and light, cachet, the borrowing of another life, play-acting while the darling peasants do one's bidding—all this buffooning parody. The Italy with which the world is enamoured is a figment, a stage set, it represents—'

'About the same percentage of the "real" Italy as Broadway or Hollywood represents America. Is that what you're trying to say? I know that. The world knows that. Even so—even *knowing* that—there are those who come here to find a share of *la dolce vita*. At least they come to search for it. Be it contrived, overpriced, tarted up for tourism, be it second-hand or fifth hand, let them be. Why didn't you speak to Fellini while you had the chance?'

This last disarms her and she laughs but I don't laugh with her. Rather, I say, 'Colonists, pilgrims, exiles, Italy is not your personal property, *signora*. I think I understand your sense of territorialism, that you want this part of Tuscany to stay as it is. Or was. But nothing does, nothing can. Nothing ever has. Stayed the same. For better, for worse, things *progress*.'

'And for every move forward there is a loss. Spendthrift as a drunken sailor, society has always been blind to and voracious for *progress* and hardly notices what it costs. It costs dignity, civility, morality, tradition, family. There should be legislation preventing the selling of land to foreigners, the construction of new buildings, the licensing of existing buildings for a use other than their original purpose.' Pulling up clump after clump of weeds, heaving them over her shoulder, Antonia is finally quiet.

'Have you transferred your anguish from the war to sit on the head of every passerby? Do you see a German soldier in disguise in every stranger? It seems as if you do. The war is over. As Luce said, no enemies muster in the hills. But they might as well for all your insisting on keeping your Breda loaded and aimed while you salt your wounds.'

'What do you know about a Breda?'

'Not much. As you so smartly put it earlier, I've never lived through a war.'

'I'll be going now, to get these little things rinsed and . . .'

'This obsession with the Occupation, could it be that you're one of those whose best days were lived during a war? Exhilaration, camaraderie, making peace with destiny, does life without war seem . . . ?'

Miss Antonia is already standing, then walking away. She stops to take her bursting sack and holds it low, nearly dragging it along the ground.

'And I don't write *buffooning parody*,' I shout after her.

Without turning towards me, she shouts back, '*A domani*. Until tomorrow.'

CHAPTER VI

Summer

It's still night and the wind is an oboe lisping through the olive trees. In the shivery blue dark I wait for her halfway up the white road between Castelletto and the lodge. There has never been a plan for this rendezvous and yet we both know the other one will be there. Walking, poking about in one meadow or another or in the woods, hardly talking at all, it's as though I have always known her. As though I will never know her. This Antonia.

I'm back at the lodge by seven for a shower and hot milk and half the loaf that Biagino has left for me. Sometimes one or two of Giorgia's eggs broken into a little warmed cream scented with thyme or sage and poached until the cream goes thick and gold and the yolks are barely set. I eat them out of the little frying pan. I sit down to work. The glee is a child's sitting down to play. Or an older child, a twelve-year-old come from behind a deep blue curtain to polite applause. She sits on the bench in front of the piano. How big it seems, how dark the hall. She straightens her back, her dress is grey, she places her foot near the pedals, looks down at the keyboard, closes her eyes then throws back her head and plays her heart out. Absorbed, engrossed, she plays until there is only her in the great dark hall. Now I write my heart out because there is only me here in Biagio's little refuge.

Even in Venice I had half a sagging velvet sofa under a wan amber light at La Marciana, and around the corner my tiny table in the bar at Florian. The far banquette at Harry's. On San Lazzaro degli Armeni, the island of the Armenians, I wrote in the monks' library but not so often. I had no computer. In San Casciano, it was Barlozzo who, close to the hearth, set up my new system and I worked through the winters with fingerless gloves and two sweaters. We lived on whatever we could cook over the fire. My little red room at number 34 via del Duomo is my first 'office' and I know that the noises of life in the *vicolo* Signorelli below my window will someday become a serenade. A comfort. The blaspheming, whistling workmen will finish their job. I know that Fernando has begun to tame his expectations. On the weekends now, it's he who speaks of the *new regime*, how we'll arrange things when I come home.

I know another thing. That beast who visits from time to time is *restlessness*. I'd worried that, having stayed away so long from my writing life, I'd lost my grit. Lost my way. That I would never again be able to *throw my head back and play with all my heart*. I should have known better.

I work until noon and eat again, or not, sit back down to work or climb up onto the princess bed to read the new pages. Sometimes Biagio finds me still at work at five and he blows a kiss, whispers, *Brava*. Mostly, though, I'm bathed and dressed and waiting for him. After tea I head for the village to shop.

My lodge cuisine has remained rustic, simple. Pasta with oil, cheese and pepper. Bread roasted in the hearth then drenched in oil or laid with cheese or *culatello* exported from Emilia. Transparent slices of artisanal *finocchiona*, wide and round as a dinner plate, I wind around stalks of white celery or small pointy green peppers, slit and seeded. Almost every day I eat beans smashed upon hot bread and topped with a few slivers of raw Tropea onion and a thread of oil. My acquisitions are so predictable that the shopkeepers begin packaging things up as soon as they see me. An *etto* of *finocchiona*, a two-hundred-gram wedge of pecorino, chestnut honey once in a while, black or red currant jam, biscuits for Biagino, heavy cream, every beautiful fruit I can find, vegetables to eat raw with oil and salt. A hundred and fifty grams of white beans.

Why don't you cook half a kilo at a time? once asked a woman I saw nearly every day in the *alimentari. It's not as though beans won't keep a week or so.*

I like to smell them cooking, I told her. *Also I like the gestures that go with fixing them: filling the pot, washing the beans, tearing the herbs, throwing in the salt. I like getting up to stir them.* She's never asked me again; she's never even talked to me since.

I visit the butcher only on Thursdays and set some small choice cut to bathe in wine and herbs and oil to be roasted on Friday evening for Fernando's supper. I buy chocolate at the *pasticceria*, Venchi 85%. I stop at the bar for a stand-up espresso or an iced Tio Pepe. Though

I see the same faces each day and they see mine, the Tuscan reserve remains unbroken. *Buona sera. Buona sera. Arrivederci. Arrivederci.* And I used to think the Orvietani were rusted shut. Sometimes Antonia and Filippa are at the bar and one of them always asks me to sit. As though my morning time with Antonia is a part of my life which I desire to keep separate from the rest, I almost always decline. As often as I'm tempted to climb the white road of an evening to join them in the kitchen, I steel myself. I focus. With something akin to giddiness, I anticipate my nightly ten o'clock call from Fernando which he makes to Giorgia and Biagio's telephone number.

All fresh and perfumed as though he's waiting for me in the flesh, I arrive at nine forty-five or sometimes earlier, sit by the fire with them, sip a glass of something, nibble at a sweet or a few roasted nuts. Standing beside the phone on the mahogany table in the hall as the clock strikes the hour, her hand poised over the receiver, Giorgia waits for the third ring before lifting it.

'*Buona sera, bello, come va?* Good evening, handsome, how are you?'

Fernando always recounts to her an event in his day, gossip from the markets, some mischief of Neddo's. When

I sense he's winding down, I go to stand perhaps a bit too close to Giorgia, fairly ready to snatch the damn phone from her just as she deigns to pass it to me. She hovers, then, a scant metre distant, her ears piqued. Though we speak briefly and mostly in code, it suffices. I stay a while longer with Giorgia and Biagio before one or both of them walks with me partway back to the lodge. Everything is ritual about these Tuscan days and nights.

'Jesumaria, *quanto freddo* . . .' I say to Antonia one morning, stamping my feet as I wait while she digs in a patch of wild garlic. Tall grasses sigh, small animals scurry. Larks wheel and I wish I'd stayed longer in the princess bed. It's seven weeks that I've been at the lodge, the last two of which have included walking with Antonia in the mornings. Seeming to have absolved me of crimes against the Tuscan peace, still she's prone to short trenchant rantings against the outlander. Though our silences are longer than our discourse, when we talk it's mostly about men and food. I like it best when we're finally resting somewhere and she starts in telling me something that happened the night before or fifty years ago. A brilliant pulpiteer, she seems a lesser listener. Or is it that she takes in what I hold back as much as what I say?

'Of course it's cold. Just like it should be at dawn on a day in June. And where did you pick up that phrase? Most Americans say *oh-my-god*, don't they? Luce says they say it twice in every sentence. She makes me laugh so when she speaks in "American". All slang, your national version of English. According to Luce, that is. So how did you come by *Jesumaria*?'

'Does it offend you? I'm sorry if—'

'No, no. I don't accuse you of *bestemmia*, of taking the Lord's name in vain, it just seems out of character for a stranger.'

'It predates my Italian days. By years and years. Giuseppe Tomasi di Lampedusa.'

'None less than he?'

'When the prince makes love to his wife, well . . . at the moment of ravishment—I have never understood whether it was hers or his or a collective ravishing—she always says *Jesumaria*. Somehow it stayed with me. I think I must have been sixteen the first time I read it. I suppose I wanted to be her. I wanted don Fabrizio to make love to me. I wanted a reason to say *Jesumaria*. Anyway, that's where it came from.'

'Poor Jesù.'

Though she's smiling, I still worry that I've blundered. 'I wouldn't have thought you were *credente*, a believer. I mean . . .'

'I'm not. I was still a girl when I decided that the three-step dance of Mother Church didn't suit me.'

'Three-step?'

'Guilt, expiation, forgiveness. The same three steps over and over. For missing mass, for murder, for, for every heinous act known to man, including eating meat on Fridays, all one must do to remain in the bosom of the Church is to confess. And if one lies in the confessional, one can always add the lie to the next batch of sins. It didn't seem fair to me. Still less by now. But that hardly means I don't have great affection for Jesus. An extraordinary boy. He'll never grow older in my eyes. I can never recall which sonnet it was . . . *To me, fair friend, you never can be old, for as first your eye I eyed, such seems your beauty still.* For me, he will always be thirty-three, carrying that cross. How many times in my life have I wanted to comfort him, to put him to bed as I would my child, cover him with sheets smelling of rosemary and thyme, push back all that hair with the flat of my hand, kiss his forehead and tell him *It's alright now*. It's strange but I never think to ask him for anything since I am already embarrassed by my own abundance. The crops cut, the wine in the barrels, the cheese wrapped and set to age, the lambs nestling against their mothers, my own in various stages of merriment and angst just as they should be . . . I've often wished I could tend to Jesus. The real flesh-and-blood man who was Jesus. If you ask me, I think he was more a lone wolf than a shepherd. Perhaps the two are much the same sort of character. In any case, the poor child never had much of a chance, what with a virgin for a mother, the God of all gods for a father and then this sweet but—in the scheme of things—ineffectual *padrino*—stepfather—who just wanted to teach him how to work with wood. Then all that wandering about trying to tell people what they should be thinking and doing and believing, when the sad truth is that each one of us must make his own way to understanding those things. Understanding them or putting them aside. Putting them aside and moving forward. In either case, it's a lonely road. His father must have known that and so why he imposed such a thankless task on that beautiful boy I can't imagine. Too—as his father must have known they would—there came betrayals and envy and the sort of hate which fear raises up. And then Jesus' denying himself what might have been true love with the Magdalena. A merciless death insufficient to redeem the sins of man, his father then sent along his other arm, the cleansing fire of the Holy Ghost, but even that didn't change much. If Jesus had been born in these times, he might well have refused to do his father's bidding. Struck out on his own. I wish he had. For all the good his dying brought down, I wish he'd told him no, packed his bag and gone off. Yes, I've often wished that for Jesus.'

Eyes closed, her hands working through the grasses, she stays quiet for a moment. I watch her, hoping she'll start talking again, but she doesn't. When she opens her eyes, all she says is, 'The beans.'

Walking double time, she explains she'd set a pot of fresh *borlotti* on the veranda burner. 'I left a note in the kitchen but who knows if any one of them . . . Come with me, and after I've seen to the beans we can go back out again.'

When we reach the villa kitchen, Filippa is there mashing the fat red-marbled beans with the end of a dowel rolling pin. Handing the bowl and the rolling pin to me, she rummages through Antonia's sack, takes out the thin stalks of garlic, the tiny buds of which she sets to work pounding to a paste in a large mortar. She takes over the mashing from me then, adds the paste and, with drops of oil and generous pinches of sea salt, works the mass to the silky texture of a mousse. She hands me two red-skinned onions. 'Would you mind?'

'How fine?' I ask, moving to the chopping block, choosing a knife.

'Fine enough. I'll put the Bialetti on. Are you hungry?' She's filling the espresso maker, toasting bread over the fire, warming milk. 'You can just throw the onions over the beans, drizzle on a little oil, cover the bowl with that cloth and set it in the pantry. Giorgia's making sausages—with the beans and a few *bruschette*, a nice lunch. Of course you'll stay.'

'It's not quite seven in the morning and I . . .'

Antonia is washing weeds. Luce enters from somewhere behind the scenes, an arm about the shoulders of a young woman who must be her daughter, so alike are they.

'Ah, Marlena, *buongiorno*,' Luce says, beaming at me, then at the young woman. 'Meet my Sabina.'

'A pleasure, I . . .'

Appearing from yet another door, Isotta interrupts, gathers Luce and Sabina and me in a hug, goes to kiss the back of Antonia's head, begins to set out cups and saucers, tiny silver spoons, yellow plates with red roses on the rims. All of them speak at once and yet everyone seems to hear and respond while not missing a beat in her own discourse. As usual I stand back, watch, listen until—swinging wide one of the veranda doors with her hip—another of them arrives.

A great pink pastry box hung from her wrist, a sheaf of red tulips wrapped in florist's paper in the crook of the other arm, she is a young Antonia. Every slope and curve and bone in her face is identical to Antonia's. I remember Filippa saying: *Viola is my elder. She's a beauty in much the same way that Antonia is. It's a fatal gift, I think. Their sort of beauty. The imperfect kind, the kind that lasts forever.*

'Bonjour, *mes petites*,' she sing-songs. '*Sei con le mandorle, sei con il miele*—six with almonds, six with honey . . . Oh, Marlena, yes?'

'Yes, I . . .'

Handing the tulips to her sister, Viola says, 'Isa, is Magda coming down? These are her favourites . . . couldn't resist them in the market . . .'

Meaning to hold out her now freed hand to me, I think, rather Viola holds out the pink pastry box, still attached to her wrist, and when I try to take it, the paper ribbon twists, slides off the box, the box crashes upon the tiles, leaving the six almond, six honey in a heap at my feet.

'I'm so sorry, I . . .'

But one of them has already whisked the pastries onto a plate while Viola has pulled me into an embrace. 'Let me look at you,' she says. Holding me at arm's length then, 'I've wanted so much to . . .'

Six of them in the kitchen is almost too much for me. All tall and blue-eyed, husky-voiced, their manes of brown-black-grey curly hair left loose or tokenly subdued in some form of chignon. All except Luce's. Antonia in her brown dress and her tool belt, the others in jeans or riding pants, t-shirts, sweaters, boots, they are all beautiful.

The seventh arrives sniffling, hair trussed up in a white towel, jeans, white shirt, ankle boots with high thick heels. Hugging, pinching cheeks, laying backs of hands to her forehead, great-grandmother, grandmother, mother, aunts, the six huddle about Magdalena, one rubbing the towel over her hair, another taking off a sweater and patting it about her shoulders, someone else pushing her into a chair, handing her an almond croissant. This is the first time I've seen all seven together and it looks like a reunion of dark-haired Virna Lisi doubles. It's *Little Women*. Another kind of no-man's land. My hands clasping the butcher's block behind me, I stand and stare. It's Magda herself who parts the crowd and comes to me, slips an arm around my waist, leads me to the table to sit next to her.

'I wish there was at least one more in my generation. Someone with whom I could *share* them. Tell me about you.'

'Nothing to tell. The most exciting part of my day is digging weeds with Antonia. I . . .'

'You've become friends. She told me that.'

The others are scattering, off to begin their days as Giorgia arrives with a basket of cabbages and platter of raw sausages.

'These need to be pierced and soaked in white wine. And the cabbages rinsed and sliced. Did anyone hear me?'

An abridged work session, a long shower and a short nap later, I am back at Castelletto, sitting with Antónia in the *salone*. It's high noon, and from a small white pitcher she is pouring peach juice into two flutes of pale amber sparkling wine.

'And don't you dare call this a Bellini. First of all, the peaches were ripe and sweet and picked this morning and the wine is a moscato from Asti rather than some half-sour mess from the Veneto.'

'Bellini would have never come to mind,' I tell her, taking a second, longer sip.

Once again, she is the small girl settling in to resume our playtime. 'I don't know very much. I think there's more light in the womb and in the grave than there is out here. Even so, every now and then I roam another time into the mists, look about for something to learn. I nearly always end up telling myself that what I don't know may not be worth knowing. What I *do* know seems to be enough. Enough so that I'm not in constant combat with life or with my portion of it. Or with those who are living it with me. I said not in *constant* combat. You may have a hard time believing that.'

'Not so hard.'

'I never did aspire to happiness in the way most people do. I feel good or I feel bad. And when I feel good I make myself remember feeling bad and when I feel bad I think about feeling good and so neither sentiment takes hold for very long. You see, I trust both. Yes, I think pleasure in great draughts would be a burden. I'm happy with my spade and my knife. I guess what I'm saying is that I like my life. I know I am nothing more nor less than a single and fleeting edition of all the fine and the less fine traits and impulses which have been passed on to me. Ancestral legacies, gifts from being born Tuscan rather than being born someone else. The power of these not to be denied and, less, the power of what I, myself, have made of these. I am taking my turn here and I am grateful for it, comfortable in my skin. Comfortable enough.

'When I hear the beards rustling on the grain I know it's ripe and that as soon as the moon is right, there'll be a week of roaring machines and four more at table, the same men who've been harvesting with us since they were boys. And on the evening when the work is done, the wheat cut and threshed and ready for the mill, those chaff-whitened faces, those descendants of the ancients who raised up the first grain from barren fields, they'll start in chanting hymns to Demeter, passing the wine jugs, laughing and yelping in their own humble kind of triumph. Olympian in its way. Not for sport but for another year's worth of bread. And right upon that stiff gold stubble, we'll set stones for a firepit, lay tables with bowls and platters and fruit and wildflowers and—the barrels near to hand, the mandolins plinking—we'll make our supper in the firelight.'

I want to tell her what I learned about the harvesting of the wheat during that long-ago summer in Sicily. And about the way the San Cascianese celebrated the harvests and to tell her that I know the hymn to Demeter . . . *I begin to sing of rich-haired Demeter, awful goddess . . .* She's quiet now and I could begin to tell her how I love these *feste*, the symbols, the rituals, that I set my own supper table on a just-cut field, straw motes riding every breeze and settling in our hair and on the sweat-shined skin of our faces and I want to tell her that . . . But she's already on to figs.

'At the first dull thump of a fig crashing onto brittle leaves I know it's time to get the kettle on, measure out the sugar. Boil the jars. When I reach for one of the fine black figs from the bowl of them on my table,

I understand that another woman might have a prettier bowl, a nicer bowl set on a lovelier cloth, that where she sits the sun might glitter through a wider window dressed with something more opulent than my fraying lace fluttering in the September breeze. I understand that another hand might be smoother than mine, the rings twining its fingers grander than my own, that another woman might have had greater loves or deeper sorrows, that she might be the Empress of India—is there such a person? I'm sure I don't know but I do like the sound of that title and I think I might like her, too—as long as she didn't want to buy up an old farmhouse and . . . But back to that fig. It's my pleasure in anticipating that fig . . . it's that *pleasure* which makes me fortunate. As I reach for the fig, I notice all of this, notice *it*, how it feels in my hand, that its perfume is like just-cracked pepper and black honey warmed by the fire. I lift it onto a small red and yellow plate, eye the fork and the pearl-handled knife set down on either side of it. Choose to bite the fig directly. Skin and all. The juices filling my mouth and bathing my chin, dripping here and there on the bosom of my dress, I've had a ceremony. It's that *sensitivity* to life, that . . .'

'*Sensitivity* perhaps. More I'd say it's *sensualità. Voluttuosità.* Sensuality. Voluptuousness.' Looking straight at her, I say the two words slowly. 'Not *unfamiliar* emotions. I mean, even to those of us not born Tuscan.'

She does her business with the tortoiseshell pins and her chignon, pushes open hands down the length of her thighs, smoothing her dress. 'It's time to give them a hand, the high-bottomed hellions.' Laughing quietly, she walks ahead, repeating *Voluttuosità*, saying it again, then again, as if it is a word she's never heard before. She turns halfway to me, says the word one more time then reaches back for my hand, pulling me forward so we walk together.

She pulls them, dark gold, thin and wide as dessert plates, from the vat of roiling oil with a wooden-handled skimmer, lays them on a soft white kitchen towel for a few seconds—long enough to rub over them crystals of sea salt between her palms, the wet salt hissing on contact with the blistering hot beauties—transfers them to a large flat basket lined with a yellow and white striped cloth. *Tortucce.* Literally, small cakes. Tuscan dialect for wild rosemary-scented flatbreads fried in the good green oil pressed from the fruit of the great-girthed olive trees parading across the hills below. The smell of the *tortucce* raises up a primal hunger, like the first hunger in the world, and my mouth waters. I swallow hard, wonder if Isotta will offer me one, but she just keeps on frying and talking, rubbing the grey salt between her beautiful brown hands—Antonia hands—plucking another plum-sized nugget of dough from her bowl and stretching it between her thumbs and fingers into a satiny disc.

'Every time I make *tortucce* I think of what Antonia told me when I was very little, about all the women who'd made them before we did. The ones fortunate enough to have a sack of flour. And a hungry family to feed. Antonia always talks about feeding people, have you noticed that? Anyhow, she would tell me that, no matter what else there was or wasn't, there was always a scruff of rosemary to be found. Salt, too. A spoonful from the jug of *biga* bubbling in the cool dimness of the pantry. I add some butter and milk to my dough, just a little, to make the crumb more tender. But they're just as good without. Antonia says *better* without. Of course, it's the oil that makes them good. Makes them *tortucce*.'

I watch and listen, wonder how many women in how many places over the past few thousand years have cooked some form of pap made of grain and water on a fired stone or in the ashes of a wood fire, a peat fire, any fire at all.

Distracted by some commotion on the other side of the terrace, she asks, 'Can you take over from me for a bit? I'll just go and help with the fritters . . .'

I finish the batch of *tortucce*, cover them—minus the one I filch—with another cloth and as I'm looking for a place to keep them warm, Antonia wanders by, takes the basket from me and begins offering them about. Someone else is already passing short tumblers full of cold *vernaccia*. When Antonia comes back my way, lifts the cloth so I can take a *tortuccia*, I tell her I can't wait to taste one. With a forefinger she flicks a betraying crumb from the corner of my mouth, says, 'The second one is never as good as the first.'

I move along the terrace to where Isotta again holds court in a narrow niche before a much smaller pan of bubbling oil set on a gas plate.

'*Frittelle di fiori di borragine*, borage-flower fritters,' she says, grinning without looking up from tossing them about. Pale blue blossoms showing through the thin gold skins of them, she lifts the fritters in a skimmer, sets them to rest in a small, cloth-lined oval basket. Another of the tribe glides by and without a word takes the basket, covers it with another cloth, carries it to the table. Whenever Isotta has the next basket ready, there is always someone there to take it. The daughters' dance is a practised one.

I step out of the terrace traffic into the greater chaos of the kitchen. At one of the five-burner stoves, Luce tosses plump pink chicken livers in butter and olive oil, sears them over a fast flame. Her thumb over the mouth of a litre bottle of *vin santo*, she splashes the livers with the dry-sweet wine, tosses the mass into a grand marble mortar. Cheeks flushed, laughing aloud at something Filippa recounts from half a hectare away, she is an alchemist grinding a wooden pestle into the steaming pluck of twenty chickens, keeping rhythm while pinching in sea salt and capers, lemon zest chopped fine as powder. Never breaking stride, she drops in bits of cold, sweet butter and droplets of cognac, pounds it all to a rough paste. A two-kilo round of charred-crusted bread she slices thinly, lays the pieces on a grate over red and white ash in a deep, flame-scorched hearth. The bread grilled on one side only, she deftly drags the untoasted side through a bowl of rich warm chicken broth and lays the bread, broth side up, on a tray. She smears the paste smoothly over the bread. Right palm upraised, she balances the laden tray on it, ports it to an iron-legged, stone-topped table set outdoors on the flags.

I wander over to Filippa as she works through a small mountain of artichokes, trimming the leaves, scraping the dread chokes—barely formed on these beauties—and peeling the nearly foot-long stems. Into each heart she presses mint leaves, crushed unpeeled cloves of garlic, thin slices of lemon, piles them up into a huge copper *bacinella*, pours in white wine, water, oil, heaves in more mint, sea salt, covers the pot and turns up the flame.

'They won't take long at all. Let's drink some wine,' she says.

On the oak dressers placed here and there against the veranda wall there are tureens of thick farro soup with new potatoes, blue and white oval platters of red wine–vinegar braised chicken and Filippa's *borlotti* mousse, its final decoration a great tangle of fried sage leaves. A wheel of young, still creamy pecorino sits on a marble near a glass bowl of caramelised peaches and another of fresh ones, some still on their leafed branches.

'*A tavola, tutti a tavola*,' invites Antonia, though she still stands—a hand folded on a hip—in front of her place at the head of the table.

From the speckled green jugs of wine passed about, everyone pours for someone else. '*Alla nostra. Alla nostra.* To us.'

Giorgia arrives with a copper tray, the sausages, charred and crackling from the fire and laid on a bed of wild rosemary branches. At the last it's Filippa and Luce—each one holding a white cloth to a handle of the steaming *bacinella* of gorgeous purple-leafed artichokes. They set it down in front of Antonia's place. From a stack of shallow soup plates before her, she takes one, places an artichoke in it, spoons on some of the lemony, winey broth from the pot, pours thick green oil over it from a two-litre *anfora*, passes it down the table.

Buon appetito echoes like a prayer.

CHAPTER VII

A roll of red-striped unbleached linen in her lap, she pulls the fabric out along the length of her arm, holds her finger to mark the place, cuts it at the mark, sets about sewing a thin, rolled hem on either end, pulling the threaded needle from where it was woven inside the pocket of her dress. It's nearly nine in the evening and Antonia and I are sitting face to face on the veranda. By the still strong light of a late June sun, she is making kitchen towels.

'The evening always astonishes me. I am far enough along so that to be able to be astonished is—in itself—a lovely thing. I come to sit here on the veranda, to look at the fields, fallow or fat, and I stay a while with a pot of some potion or other concocted from the day's harvest, tearing bread for the hens and yearning for something, yearning for everything I suppose, though I can never put a name to it. To the longing, I mean. I can't tell if it's nostalgia—someone or something I miss—or someone, something I've never known.'

Hiraeth. Perhaps it's hiraeth, Antonia, I say to myself. That Welsh word again . . . yearning, grieving, but for whom? For what?

'Is it my Tancredi? Do I still wait for him? Hindsight has led me to believe there was a certain fortune in losing him so soon, the risk of disenchantment being the greatest for the one we love best. Is it Ugo for whom I long? Surely it is. Those long legs wrapped around mine for all those nights . . . How I loved the smell of him. I wore his leather jacket until a few years ago when Isa or one of the others locked it away in some trunk. He hunted in it, rode in it and, as though the old soft skin of it had become his own, I could find him there. Cloves and pine and amber, woodsmoke. Without the jacket I can find him still.

'But more than Ugo and Tancredi, more than my father and all the others whom I loved for a while or forever, I think the *longing* I feel is to know whether I've made a good job of it. Of life. Nothing cloaked or squandered. Aiming for it, I pretend every morning is my last. Once past eighty, I think that game is just. Besides, there's a kind of thrill in it. Not at all morbid, mind you, but exhilarating, yes, that's what it is. Moving along that windblown edge where every footfall counts. It's not that I *practise* dying but, my stash of days having dwindled as it has, I sidle up closer to its inevitability. Like winter, sooner or later it will come. Wily creature, the Horseman, I'll meet him head-on, no cringing. It would be a brutal thing to hear his rough whispering, to understand it's me he's come for and then to feel my head spinning and tilting with scenes half played, played badly, words not said. Said. Having understood that a life entire is contained within every day and its night, I get on with things. As I keep telling you—and all of them—*festina lente*. Make haste slowly.'

Antonia bites the thread, folds a finished towel in three, puts it on the pile, cuts another length. Rethreads the needle. 'I guess this is as good a time as any. To begin.'

'To begin . . . ?'

'It's what you desire, isn't it? Or what the others desire. I know they've been stealthing around, asking you to lure me into storytelling.'

'Not in any but the most delicate way.'

'Is that why Luce invited you to tea at the hotel—when was it?—two days ago? To ask you to—'

'Luce and I talked mostly about her journeys to America. But yes, she did tell me she wishes you'd write your stories. Begin writing them. She thinks you would be less discreet in writing than you would be in speaking.'

'She's probably right. But I don't know if I *could* write it all down. I've never written more than a few letters in my whole life. Imagine that Madame de Somebody—I can't remember her name—who wrote all those letters to her daughter. Worse, that Bohemian Rilke, leaving ten thousand letters behind—or was it twenty thousand? Old fop. It would have been a life better spent if he'd cooked ten thousand suppers.' Putting down her sewing, she leans towards me, shakes her head. 'I don't even know if I have time to write it all down. I don't mean hours in a day but days themselves . . . How many could I have left to . . . ?'

'You could try. You could begin.'

'That's the substance, isn't it? They're fearful I'll die without having said all they want to hear.'

'Maybe they're more fearful you'll die without your saying all you long to say. *Nothing squandered, nothing cloaked.* That's what you said.'

'As for the *nothing squandered* part, that's tough but I work at it. The *nothing cloaked* part referred to myself. To telling *myself* the truth. I don't know that I long to *uncloak* much of anything to anyone else. From time to time I've tried. Speaking to Filippa, to Luce. More than once to both of them together. I never get very far. I end up leaving holes, feeling the fool, listening to myself with their ears, watching every move they make, trying to understand how they judge me. And so I censor. Only a little and then a little more and then all of it begins to fall apart and I hear myself telling someone else's stories. It never works. Poor things. They're so much older than me by now. I think I prefer to take my mysteries with me.'

'Probably best that way.'

'Probably.'

Sewing a fine seam, she stays quiet.

'Maybe not though,' she says, needle poised above the cloth.

'Maybe not.'

Having stowed her sewing things, poured out some grass-smelling concoction into two tall glasses, Antonia is tremulous as an ingénue. I taste the dark green stuff, tell her it's nothing less than disgusting. Laughing seems to calm her.

'We'll be here for a while, you know. Once I get started, well . . .'

'It's fine. As long as I don't have to drink that.'

'Well now, as far as I know—this having been told to me in starts and stops and with revisions and over time—I was born six days after the man who was my mother's husband set off to join a regiment of Alpini which was billeted up in the Friuli. A volunteer in a time of peace since there was none for him at home, I'd say. You see, for nearly nine months my mother had chosen not to reveal to him her doubts about the paternity of the child she carried. Barren for all the seven years of their marriage and cuckolding him, when she announced she was with child, he—her husband—went wild with joy. The joy of her darling swain—the man who, as she lay dying, she named the single love of her life—was less convincing. Wishing my mother good fortune, the lover moved on. With the wife of the baker in Pietrasanta, as I recall the story. I might have invented that but I don't think so. I've often wondered at my mother's suffering over the loss of her lover, if that suffering was passed on to me. I think it was. In the form of melancholy. A minor-key agony small and sharp as a pebble, it's as known to me as are my eyes.

'I haven't a single memory—early or late—of her *mothering* me. I don't mean to say she was less than diligent, that she didn't work day and night, that I lacked much of anything save a caress or two. Or her hands holding my face for a moment once in a while, her eyes on mine. What she didn't or couldn't give to me, I gave to her. A quick study, I knew when to praise and how to comfort, how to make her laugh. I learned how to rescue her. Even from herself. Not knowing then that things were reversed in a way—not knowing it might have been she who put the pebble in my shoe—the events seemed quite natural to me. Given who she was and who I am, I guess they were. I've often thought my mother was my first child.

'In any case, it must have been in a fit of prenatal putting her house in order that she told her husband the truth. *It could be yours. It could be his.* Her husband packed his valise and six days later I was born. May third, 1920. She having no family of her own, it was a woman from the village who delivered my mother with nothing more than hot water, olive oil and whispered incantations. We're as much pagan here as we are anything else. A brother of my mother's husband looked after the farm until she was strong enough to take up the work herself. I don't remember those first years save when I look at a photo—taken by whom, I never knew—of my mother with her skirts kilted up on her thighs and wearing what must have been her husband's boots, her body bent to the job of turning the soil in the wheatfield. Maybe two years old, I am close beside her, naked save white pantaloons which end below my knees, leaning on my own homemade hoe, posing for the camera.

'I was nearly three when my mother's husband returned. Whether for the love of her, or the ache that he might have abandoned a child who was, indeed, spawn of his own flesh, I do not know. Rather, though, I think it was the patriarchal call to his land, the land of his father and his father's father, that surpassed all other of his yearnings. I shall never know. What I do know is that about then—and perhaps it was *because* of his return—my childhood began. Though to this day I do not know if *he* was or if the *other one* was, from here on I shall refer to him—Marco-Tullio—as my father. I loved him, love him mightily still.

'It was just before I married that my mother began to tell me about this. In a second fit of putting things in order, I suppose. Like explaining the mechanics of the marriage bed, she said it was her *duty*. I thought her treacherous then. I have since softened that verdict, having lived long enough to enact my own treacheries and understand that we all do. Even mothers do. Most especially our own. Certain, I am *certain* she knew which man fathered me. Women always know. If she'd had a *duty* to me I should think it would have been to tell me what she knew. She died soon after I married. By then I'd understood it was right that she'd never told me. She gave me the chance to choose. I chose Marco-Tullio as my father.

'Knowing nothing of my parents' story when I was growing up, I cannot tell you that I suffered as a child. But perhaps I did. Perhaps we all do. I think we all do. Still, we lived well together, we three. Or was it that we lived as well as we three—any three—could? If ghosts moved among us, they were tranquil ones. It wasn't until I married Tancredi that I learned there was another kind of life than the one I'd lived for almost eighteen years with my parents. Life beyond the farm, beyond the work, the washing and cooking and praying and sleeping and the smell of baking bread on Saturday and roasting rabbit on Sunday. On Monday the *fiaschetto* with the wet rag stuffed in its neck so it wouldn't explode in the ashes, the green glass *fiaschetto* that held the soaked beans, a few drops of oil, a half-glass of white wine, a spoonful of tomato conserve and the four fat leaves of sage which I was sent to pick near the grapevines. I can still see my mother's hands measuring it all, hear her singing so loud my father would call her *la squarciagola*—the throat-splitter. I'd never thought about whether we were poor or not—if being *poor* had even been something I'd understood back then. By now I know that we never were. Not poor at all, save that we had no money. A few hectares of good land—that and our wits and our muscle and the grace of the angels were enough to keep us. A field for wheat and one for corn, a hillside for vines and orchards, a meadow for sheep, a small stone house for us and a stable for two cows and a mule: we had more than most. I don't recall being hungry, not very hungry and not so often hungry, though I do remember stealing into the *tinello* once when my parents were at their work. Slicing bread from the weekly loaf and pushing a badly sawed-off piece into the pocket of my dress, I ran like the wind, weaving my five- or six-year-old self pell-mell through the wheatfield, the high, dry August fronds of it scraping across my cheeks. Heading for the orchards, heart pounding in my skinny chest, giving a wide berth to the flock, I ran until I fell on my knees before the heap of broken branches from a pear tree under which I'd buried a piece of honeycomb earlier that morning. Hands shaking from want of the stuff, I swiped the bread across the amber pools that dripped from the comb and, holding the bread in the flat of my palm, I gnawed it like a starving she-wolf. It still makes the saliva run when I think of it and every time I do, I'm grateful I was able to taste the bread and honey with that kind of hunger. And with that greater hunger, too. The sensual kind which perpetrates ecstasy and misery, if not always in equal portions. But I didn't know that then. No, not then.

'But there was another reason why I was never poor. Marco-Tullio, my father, was a reader. Rare enough in those days, a farmer who knew how to read, books were his haven. As I think about it, he didn't have many he could call his own save *I Promessi Sposi*, *Cavalleria Rusticana* and *La Vita Nuova*, all three of which he read with great constancy. He borrowed books from the nuns and, when he could get there, from the Biblioteca Cimati in Pontremoli—poetry, history, classics. He would sit by the fire after supper or, when the light stayed, on a straw-seated chair among the apple trees and read until he slept. When my mother and I had finished whatever little jobs there were left to do before we went to bed, she would tell me, *Vai a svegliare Orazio*—Go to wake Horace. I would tiptoe as quietly as I could so he wouldn't wake until I touched his cheek. *Papà, è tardi*, it's late, I'd tell him and he'd follow me down the path carrying his chair or stand to stir the embers and place a night log over them. He'd always come into the alcove where my bed was, sit beside me for a moment, distil what he'd read in some fantastic fashion which he knew would suit me and that's what I'd fall asleep thinking about. Dour old Tuscan that he was, those stories were as close as Marco-Tullio ever came to an embrace.

'He taught me to read before I went to school, gifted me Salgari when I was nine, and thereafter he and I would sit together of an evening with our books. By that time it was I who'd march him off to bed, crawl into mine, never closing my eyes until the bells rang three or four. Even then I was unwilling to let life leak away while I slept.

'Not so clever a student at school, it wasn't structured learning which excited me but the kind which came from turning pages and entering deeper and deeper into other people's thoughts and lives, what they saw and felt. What shocked and thrilled me was that sometimes they were the same things I saw and felt. And so it isn't only a farmer's daughter that I am but Marco-Tullio's daughter. Marco-Tullio, alias Orazio. All this is to say, whatever time I could steal from my chores and my schoolwork, I spent reading. Reading and dreaming. I never did run about with my schoolmates, they always languishing in one titillation or another, falling into a fever over a hair bow or in love with the *ragazzo* who sold *cecina* from a truck near the school. Even so, by the time I was about fourteen—perhaps I was younger than that—I'd begun to notice him. Tancredi.

'Tall and well made, red-blond hair falling over his eyes—it was the eyes I saw first. Long and green, pale green like sea glass. I never knew eyes could be green. Anyhow, his family had a pew, the front pew on the left, at San Agostino. Though the family wasn't titled, the de Gaspari of Castelletto were the closest thing in our parts to nobility. For as far back as anyone could recall, they'd owned most of the province, keeping a small battalion of sharecroppers to work the land. And so there they'd be, the de Gaspari, all lined up in their finery like they were going to a ball: his parents; his elder brother, Ugo; cousins who lived with them; his mother's maid, even their cook and I don't know who else, but the pew was full and they the object of everyone else's gaze.

'I couldn't say who among our families was left with less breath when Tancredi made known his will to marry me. I was seventeen, Tancredi twenty and it wanted only two glances for me to understand that will. One glance when he turned around after mass one Sunday, searched the congregation for me. When he found me, he smiled, shook his head in a kind of disbelief—I think it might have been disbelief—and then smiled again. The second glance came a few days later at the market in Pontremoli. We didn't set up our table with any regularity, Mamma and I, but only when we had extra eggs or had found the time to pick field lettuces and toss them with wildflowers and cart them down in a basket. In June we would often bring peaches. A few branches heavy with the fattest, rosiest ones which she'd lay on a red glass tray—a wedding gift from her own mother—and carry it against her hip all the way down the hill. It was peaches we had that day when Tancredi walked up to us, strode right up as though Mamma and I, sitting there between the olive lady and the egg lady with our elbows tight against our bodies, were the object of his morning's mission. He asked Mamma if he could buy the peaches, handed her some *lire*, all the while looking at me. And then he walked away. Without the peaches.

'Improbable as it was, I'd expected him to proceed with his curious sort of courtship, to speak to me in church, to visit the market again. But Tancredi dispensed with preludes and arrived at dusk on an evening in late June driving a one-horse carriage and wearing a straw *borsalino*.

We'd been shearing sheep, my father and I, me holding while he clipped. I smelled of lanolin and sweat and likely of sheep's blood from all the nicks my father left on their white shuddering bodies. I was in the *orto* picking broad beans for supper and I heard him, saw him drive up. I saw him descend and I ran. Dropping the hem of my skirt, the beans tumbling before me, I ran barefoot right in front of him and into the house and I could hear him laughing as he ladened his arms with wine bottles and a cheese wrapped in thick white cloth. From the window upstairs I watched him sit on the veranda steps, set down the bottles and the cheese, arrange them in one design and then in another as he waited, straightening his jacket, taking off his hat and smoothing his hair and then putting the hat back in place. Soon enough my father came loping along the path through clumps of wild sage, and Tancredi stood.

"*Buona sera, signor* Ducchi."

'He asked my father for my hand. Pure and simple in his sober Tuscan way he asked and, pure and simple in *his* Tuscan way, my father answered. I seemed the only one incredulous. Why me? Why did Tancredi, the gallant of three counties, he who might have increased his father's riches by aligning himself with a family from as far away as Firenze, why did he want me?'

Poor Tancredi, I think, looking at her, imagining Antonia as she must have been just coming into bud. He'd never had a chance.

'Marry we did. During the week between Christmas and the New Year. I in Tancredi's mother's lynx cape over an old-rose-coloured dress that was also hers, a tiara of the tiniest callas he'd ordered from a *fioraia* in Liguria, as I recall. Imagine that. He wore riding clothes. He always did. That day with an ivory satin cravat. High mass at twilight on a Tuesday, the church was empty save us, our parents, his brother. Yes, Ugo was there, I'd forgotten that. Ugo. His elder brother. I'll get to him.

'Certain I'd wanted to marry this Tancredi, I was at the same time loath to leave the farm. Mostly to leave Marco-Tullio. I was frightened at least as much as I was intrigued. There'd been neither time nor funds to furnish me with a trousseau and I remember ransacking drawers and cupboards trying to find enough belongings to some-what fill the slightly used, odd little pale yellow leather trunk my parents had bought for me. Two work dresses, a Sunday one, a winter coat—third-generation black with a brown collar and an old-lady smell about it—nightdresses, underthings. Boots and shoes and woollen stockings. Books. Still there was enough room for me to crawl into, and I was moved to lay flat round stones gathered from the creekbed over the bottom of the yellow trunk. At least it would be heavy, I thought. At least that.

'When Tancredi came to fetch me on the afternoon before the wedding—that was how he'd arranged things with my father—and brought me to Castelletto, his parents and his brother, the servants, the farm workers, everyone stood in the hall to greet me. Tribute to their collective affection for Tancredi, they welcomed me as though I were a long-awaited fairy princess, as though I'd come to wed them all. Having spent my first seventeen years in a household of three, life at Castelletto seemed a festival of characters in constant motion. Upstairs maids, downstairs maids, gardeners, seamstresses, handymen. A flush-faced, mustachioed cook with one blue eye, one brown, named Edoarda. A head housekeeper who was also a kind of lady-in-waiting to my mother-in-law—her confidante too, I think—Abriana. And Abriana's daughter, Tessa she was called, a thin, dark-skinned girl of ten with black Tartar eyes and two thick plaits like shiny whips flying behind her as she ran about. Though my mother had warned they would, no one pursed his lips over Tancredi's choosing an undowried *contadina* for a wife. None that I noticed. Maria-Luce, Tancredi's mother, and Battista, his father, became and remain idols for me. I don't know who or what I loved most during those early days . . . was it Tancredi? Was it the household entire? Was it that I loved *being* loved? I think it was.

'At the beginning they must have found me coarse in my ways, Maria-Luce and Battista—perhaps even Tancredi. But I think they were at least as much stimulated by me. I felt loving towards his parents and so I showed it. Ignoring ceremony, I would hug and kiss them, look in their eyes and hold their fine smooth faces in my hands, all the gestures I'd longed to make towards my own parents and to have them make to me. They responded in kind, emboldening me. I became as much theirs as I was Tancredi's. For the first time, I was a child. Beloved, cherished. Years passed before I began to understand that wasn't so at all. It was Marco-Tullio's affection—less overt, of another ilk—that formed me. In the same way that my father made the path for me to books, he gave me the sense that I was *amabile*, loveable. Until this day I don't know a more important gift to give a child. Surely it sustains above all others.

'And so that first era of my life here at Castelletto seemed, at the time, an idyll of sorts. Whether it was, well, between what's true and what's real, there is always some stretch of wilderness. Years after, it was Ugo who told me of the sadness between Maria-Luce and Battista, their marriage having been a bow to familial duty. *One reason why they rejoiced when Tancredi chose you*, he'd said. *Perhaps also one reason why he* did *choose you.*

'Correct, sensitive, Maria-Luce and Battista invited my parents to come and stay at Castelletto, to attend every social event at the villa, sent them gifts, arranged for me to be driven often to visit them. Still, I soon became a stranger to them, there being no bridge between where I'd been and where I'd gone. By now I am certain my parents were relieved by my absence, happy surely that I'd landed well but also, yes, *relieved*. Finally they were free to behave with one another as they felt, their witness gone away. At forty-seven, and less than a year after my wedding, my mother died. *Female complications* were named the cause. As I told you, her last words were about her lover. A brief and echoing tale, the human story.

'It was three months after my eighteenth birthday—a sultry day in August 1938—when Maria-Luce accompanied me to visit her doctor in Pontremoli, he confirming what we two had calculated and kept secret. The creature I was carrying would be born in February. On the veranda that evening I told my news to Tancredi. Saying not a word, he laid his hand on my still unswelled *pancettina*, those sea-coloured eyes finding mine; it was the only time I saw him weep.

'About then the cravings began. Not for things to eat but for things to cook. It had been months since I'd put my hands to supper, to all the magic that could come of peeling a few onions and pulling the spikes from a branch of rosemary, mincing them together and setting the pulp to stew in a little hot oil. I cajoled Maria-Luce into granting me kitchen time. Though she found the request perplexing, she agreed. At first, I could only be in there with the cook, she doing most of the work, assigning me the dainty tasks. Glossing a tart. Dusting the bread tins with cornmeal or slicing the half-baked loaves of *cantucci* and arranging the pieces on an oven tray. I soon took things into my own hands. One morning when Cook and Maria-Luce came strolling into the kitchen for their daily meeting I was at the sink, busy with slitting the throat of a rabbit I'd thieved from the hutch. Shrilling and screaming over the impropriety of Tancredi's bride bloodying her hands with such work *just like a common peasant*, Maria-Luce stopped short her tirade, nearly choking on her gaffe. A common peasant being exactly who I was. While Cook was relieving me of the limp little carcass, wiping my hands with a cloth she'd wet from the kettle, Maria-Luce was holding me close, her screams having turned to soft laughter. We sat at the work table then and Cook fixed me a breakfast of wild sage tea with an egg yolk beaten in and poured over roasted bread. Snorting and tsk-tsk-ing about the room, she kept repeating, *That poor unborn creature is marked, no question about it. An assassin is the best we can hope for now.* Sitting close to me, watching me spoon up the good soup, Maria-Luce asked, *Did you wish to cook the rabbit, Antonia? I mean, did you really wish to cook it yourself?*

'Little by little I worked my way into the kitchen until I was spending so much time there that Maria-Luce, feeling excluded, joined Cook and me, all three of us with our hands in the flour. Telling stories. Even now when I cook with the hellions I think back on those mornings with Maria-Luce. We laughed and sang and we made wonderful food. I'd fix a dish, then Cook would, and sometimes Maria-Luce did, too. Well, not so much *cook* it as talk about it. She would start in remembering what she liked as a child, tell us how it tasted, how it looked, how it smelled, and Cook and I would get to work. One morning we made one of those dishes from her memory and I loved it so much I still cook it every chance I get. I can still hear her girlish voice saying, *Well, it was a soup but thicker, kind of like polenta is while it's still warm, and it had fennel, wild fennel—I'm sure of that. But it was made of verza, yes, the base was a green verza. Beautiful with those great floppy leaves, I remember. But it was* piccante, *spicy, but not so much that it burned. Could there have been garlic? And some other herb. I can taste the herb but I can't say what it was. Oregano? Marjoram?* As she talked I poured oil into a pot, more than just enough to cover the bottom, always a little more than you might think necessary. Always over a medium flame. That's the Tuscan way to cook with olive oil. Having crushed a handful of wild fennel seeds with the flat of a knife, I scraped them into the warmed oil. Between my palms, I rubbed in the dried buds from two small branches of *origano*, and a fat, dried red *peperoncino*. Next, a few purple-skinned cloves of garlic, peeled, smashed, minced to a paste and, finally, between the palms once more, I rubbed in crystals of sea salt and left the mass to stew over a low flame. When it sent up its perfume, I added the *verza*, sliced thinly, stirred it all around in that scented oil. I covered the pot, let the cabbage go soft. *And what else? What else was in it?* I'd asked her, already knowing what I was going to do next. I took hardened bread—about a half-kilo—from the tin box where Cook kept it for *ribollita* and *acquacotta*, and tossed it into the pot while both of them shouted at me that I must soak leftover bread before . . . Never minding them, I added two litres of water, another generous pour of oil, covered the pot and simmered it all until the bread and the cabbage were soft. Then I called for cooked white beans, and Cook, shaking her head, took a litre jar from the *tinello*. Twisting her apron around the jar's metal cap, she opened it, handed it to me, sat down, elbows on the table, head leaning on her hands, lamenting that her kitchen had been commandeered by a long, tall farmer's daughter. I stirred, she fretted and Maria-Luce laughed. I passed the soup through a sieve and ribbons of pale green silk fell into the big white bowl. Taking a small spoon, scraping it across the surface of the pap, I offered

it to Maria-Luce. *How did you know?* she asked. Truth was
I didn't know, but since beans and bread and cabbage
were and are everyday foodstuffs here, it was a fairly
safe guess that these played in her taste memories. And
so I used them all. Cook tasted it, too, and, still shaking
her head, half smiled, poured some into the tureen for
lunch, the rest into litre jars to cool in the *tinello*. There
was still some clinging to the sides and the bottom of the
bowl and, without agreeing to, each of us tore a small
crust from the *pagnotta* that was set out for lunch, skated
it across the soup, tossed the crust into our mouths, tore
off another piece of crust and repeated the communion.
Soon Cook went back to the pantry, returned with a jar of
the soup and poured out another centimetre or two into
the bowl. We tore and skated and slurped until Battista
and Tancredi and Ugo came into the kitchen to find out
why we weren't at table. Finding it easier to demonstrate
than to explain, we tore crusts for each one, urging them
on until all six of us were huddled around the bowl, the
pagnotta by then reduced to soft whitish innards shorn of
its crackled, charred crust. Another *pagnotta* was brought
forth, the soup ladled into warmed bowls, threads of oil
poured over it, spoons and napkins laid for what was to

become an historical lunch, the first one the de Gaspari had ever eaten in the kitchen. All this talk, doesn't it make you hungry?'

'It does. Hungry not just for soup and bread but hungry to have *been* there. I think it makes me more hungry for that.'

'Then let's cook while we talk. Let's eat while we talk. No use doing one thing at a time when we can do two or three. *Nothing squandered.*'

'With the daughters, of course.'

'With the daughters.'

CHAPTER VIII

In the early evenings Antonia and I, together with some formation of the daughters, set out on the work table what there was to be cooked, considered the elements, more or less agreed on what dishes to make and who would make them. How many pots did we rattle about over the flames in that hearth and on the burners of those stoves, how many more did we nestle in the seething red ash of an olive-wood fire to simmer while we sat around the table listening to Antonia, taking turns whittling a kilo wheel of pecorino and pouring out fennel tea from a big blue pot, or *vernaccia*, cold and clean, from the green-speckled pitcher? And when the moment seemed right, we'd sip good-enough whisky, burgled by one of the daughters from Antonia's lingerie chest, from the flask she always hid beneath the peach satin culottes which Luce swore were hers, had always been hers and which Antonia, in a rage of nubile-daughter envy, had confiscated nearly forty years before. An unresolved question, the peach satin culottes were between Antonia and Luce.

Filippa or Luce likely having warned the others that Antonia was not to be interrupted in her soliloquies, there was, at first, a kind of stilted silence among the daughters. But it didn't last long. After a session or two, whoever had one asked a question, interjected, expressed awe or disdain or laughed or wept. Not too many evenings passed before all six of the daughters scurried to convene in the kitchen punctually as for mass. Giorgia, too.

Mostly to accommodate the schedules of Viola and Isotta and Magdalena, the hour of our meeting grew later and later so that, from wherever each one had spent the afternoon, we'd arrive at the villa just as the light was fading to blue and the black limbs of the oaks made lace against the sky. Sometimes I'd be carrying a sack of one thing or another brought up from the village or Filippa

and I would set about picking *borlotti*, barely able to see
the bean stalks in the leaving light, she calling out to
Viola as we neared the house, telling her to put the pot
to boil on the veranda stove while Luce and Antonia and
Isotta would be dawdling arm in arm through the pines
on their way back up the sea path, one of them swinging
a basket of cones for the fire. There was always a fire,
even in July.

We'd set about changing shoes, lifting dresses or
sweaters over our heads, rearranging the shifted flesh of
our bosoms back into our brassieres and tying on one
of the pinafores which hung in a tangle on a black iron
hook by the back door and always smelled of thyme. We'd
throw open the windows to the night, swaddle the rising
bread with quilts against the breeze.

It was Filippa who minced about in Antonia's velvet
sabots, a tribal sacristan lighting every candle in the
place. On the claw-foot mahogany bench in front of the
baby grand, Isotta would sit to play, Filoush curled in her
lap, his front paws covering his ears against her melancholy ripples. Midst Isotta's tinkling and the chinking of
bowls and the rhythm of knives, Antonia would begin.
Fixing and unfixing the tortoiseshell pins in her hair,

waving those long brown hands like a benign witch with a wand, she held them in thrall, the daughters. No less Giorgia, no less me.

When Antonia seemed to grow tired, her voice dwindling to a whisper so the only sounds were Isotta's melody and the hiss of juices dripping into the flames, one of us would fill the interval, pretend something was about to burn, to boil over, get up to rinse glasses, wash a dish. But she would rally, Antonia. Tell us things we'd forgotten or mistaken or would never understand about food, about men, about the panacea of bitter weeds, the glories of she-ass milk for the skin. About herself.

When someone else desired to speak, she did. Weeping, whispering, trying out the sounds of a truth, a secret, candles shuddering as the doors opened, closed again. Open. Close. An ageing feminine chorus ornamented with the single nymph that was Magdalena, we carried on against the flickering light.

Oh, the men were there, in and out, sometimes sitting a while with a glass of wine while we worked and talked— Biagio, Umberto, Magdalena's Giangiacomo, Guglielmo on the weekends, often one of Luce's gentlemen friends. And Fernando, too. Antonia herself had come down to the lodge one Friday evening and invited him to join us. I having already explained to Fernando about the evenings with Antonia, about my not wanting to miss any of them, but wanting less for him to be displeased if we renounced the privacy of our weekends, her intervention was welcome. I can't say who between them charmed the other one most, Antonia flirting with Fernando, he slipping into gallantry as only a Venetian can.

That first meeting between them would lead to Antonia's convincing me that Fernando should indeed stay with me at the lodge, that it wasn't good for us to be separated for so long, that since my routine of work and play was so well established, his presence should now be welcome. *Besides*, she'd said, *it will be good for Biagio and Umberto to have another resident male. Good for all of us. Do you think he'd be willing to stay?* Willing he was and so he did.

But the men of Castelletto had their own place to be while the women cooked and talked. At the top of a long spiral staircase, a room of their own tucked up under the eaves of the attics, the *mansarda*, it had the good smells of men just bathed and perfumed, of freshly ironed shirts, polished boots, the fumes of honest red wine and the black-rum haze of a thousand pipes smoked in sainted peace. Sometime later, Antonia would tell me of other men who, long ago and for a while, wore another kind of boots up there under the eaves. Left behind another kind of perfume.

By the time supper was served it was well past ten, or often later. It was the way Antonia liked it so the time around the table would stretch beyond midnight and she'd have only four hours or so to stay put in her bed. Biagio and Giorgia would keep to their own rhythms, say their good evenings after the soup and go off to their beds, but the others, most of them, followed Antonia's pace, eating and drinking, in no hurry for the time together to end. Almost bridal on those evenings, Antonia was languid, clucking gently about her fine candlelit parish. More than once I thought, *I would be missing all of this had Luce not called me back, had I walked away down the white gravel road carving an x on the name of Antonia Ducchi de Gaspari. When to carve the x, when to keep the knife in your pocket? Where sits the boundary?*

Evening after evening, Antonia spoke about the first days of her marriage to Tancredi, her always-growing affection for Maria-Luce and Battista, about beginning to prepare for her baby's arrival, *quella creatura che stavo crescendo dentro di me*, the creature who was growing inside me. Endearing stories, affectionately told. Entrenched there, Antonia would recall another, then another scene in that long-ago August.

It is Magda who stops her once midway through some *racconto*. 'Nonnina, but what happened *after* that . . . ?'

'After? Well, I guess it got to be September. The *vendemmia*, the . . .'

The daughters, knowing well enough about the grapes, send up a collective moan.

'It's my story. I'll tell it as I wish.. And at the pace I wish. No one is obliged to listen. I was going to tell you about the *vendemmia* on our farm. When I was a girl. That's what I was going to tell you. Anyone who'd rather not be here, now's the time to go.'

No one moves.

'My mother, my father and I, along with six or eight or—when the yield was great—as many as a dozen neighbours, could cut the grapes and begin the maceration in a single day. Lighting a fire in the stone pit to warm ourselves, we'd sit under the stars drinking from the barrel we'd saved for the occasion from the last year's vintage. Then we'd offer to the helpers what was, for us, a notable supper. We laid translucent slices of lard perfumed with wildflowers and aged in marble vats in the caves near Colonnata over trenchers of bread roasted on sticks, a thick soup made with bread and tomatoes and red wine and tiny leaves of wild basil which we'd set down for a long slow session in the wood-fired oven. Wild or home-raised—as our fortunes permitted—there was always some part of a pig which my father had set to bathe in a potion of wine and herbs and oil in a scorched earthen pot. Burying it in the embers of the stone pit the evening before the harvest, leaving it to braise through the night until, when we scraped away the still-warm ash and took off the lid next morning, the flesh had fallen from its bones and mingled with the woodsmoke and, I suppose, all the other good things that had cooked in that pot for who knows how many years. I still have it, by the way, that old *coccio*. I use it for something or other every day. The truly immoderate part of our feast, though, was the ending. The apples fried in white wine batter. It was my job to pick the apples, drag them home from the orchards in sacks, core and peel ten kilos or so, slice them into thick rounds, plunge them into the batter and then the oil. I'd let them float about until they were all dark and golden, and while they were still burning hot I'd roll them in sugar wet with rum so it would stick only here and there and make a kind of glaze on the fritters. And when there was enough batter, I fried the peel as well, slicing it thinly and throwing it in the oil every which way. Retrieving it in tangles with a strainer, giving it a good roll in sugar, this—even more than the apples themselves—was what everyone waited for. I used to love how quiet it became as they set to gorging on the sweets. A breeze rustling the shorn vines, the squeaking of a few nightbirds and, every once in a while, a softly beseeched *Dio buono*. Good God.

'The next morning, just after the dew was dry, the troupe—including us—would be off to harvest another farm, on and on for a week or more until everyone's grapes were in. A more homespun harvest, ours.

'Back then as now, the harvest at Castelletto lasted for days, each vineyard on the estate picked when its particular grape was ripe. The *fattore* was the judge. When the September moon began to wax, the *fattore* and his crew would go out at sunrise each morning and stand near a vine. The *fattore* would pluck a grape, a single grape, his face already arranged in disdain. He'd drop it into his open maw, chew it, move the pulp of it around in his mouth for a time. Then he'd spit. Shaking his head, he'd turn back to the day and its work and that was that. Next morning, the same performance. Until, on one of those mornings after he'd chewed on the grape, he didn't spit but held both arms out straight like a scarecrow, making scissors of his fingers, and the men would send up a hallelujah. But the *sangiovese* was always last. The *fattore* always waited, giving the fruit one more dose of hot September sun, one more day to bring up the sugar, *Only one more day*, he would say each morning, until the fat black fruit was dripping with the blood of Giove himself.

'Tancredi already in the fields, I was still asleep when Maria-Luce came to fetch me on the morning of that first *vendemmia* of my life at Castelletto, telling me to come quickly with her into the vineyards, saying, *They can't cut until we do. Hurry.* Understanding nothing, buttoning Tancredi's sweater over my nightdress, stepping into my boots, I ran. Baskets at their feet, secateurs in hand, hats turned down against the sun, all the farmers waiting, grinning, shaking their heads, wishing me *buongiorno*,

I followed Maria-Luce among the vines. She would stop, inspect the fruit, go a little further, inspect again. Finally she nodded. The *fattore* handing her a pair of secateurs and she positioning them for cutting the great heavy bunch she'd chosen, she told me to put my hand over hers. Taking a deep breath, she whispered words I didn't understand, told me to hold tight as she severed the grapes. The farmers cheered, a woman stepped up with a white cloth in which she cradled the just-cut grapes and then went running off with them. Maria-Luce stood there with her arms around me for the longest time.

'"The first grapes are for the *schiacciata*," she said. "We lay the fruit on flattened, spiced bread dough and bake it in the wood oven. *Schiacciata con l'uve.* In small pieces, we'll offer the bread to the workers this evening with a glass from a barrel of last year's wine. Communion. And when I'm no longer, it will fall to you to cut the grapes with your youngest daughter. No matter how many men in the family, it is always female to female, the ceremony."

'Back then there were eighty, maybe a hundred souls cutting the Castelletto grapes and half that many cooking and baking to feed them three times a day. But on the evening when the harvest was in, tables were set up between the shorn vines on the lowest terraces, lanterns lit, torches pummelled into the soft, trampled earth and an endless supper was served. Maria-Luce kept me out of the kitchen and close to her, introducing me to the extended family who, not having made the journey when Tancredi and I were wed, had come to celebrate from as far as Roma. It was on that evening when Maria-Luce began to say goodbye.

'I remember the moon was a great white flower blooming up from the mountains and the night mists were succulent, wet with the smell of grapes. After supper, the men having gone off to smoke, to throw the *bocce* down the oak walk, Maria-Luce and I sat at a table with some of the other women. Though there was animated talk, Maria-Luce was quiet, distracted. One arm leaning on the table, with the other she tugged my arm downward, took my hand, held it, swinging it to and fro every now and then or squeezing it. We stayed like that for a long time, breaking apart only to dip another crust of bread in our wine. We'd put our hands right back where they were then, as though holding on to each other was what we did always. I remember her asking me if I wanted to stretch my legs a bit and I said I did. Arm in arm, we walked in the torchlight up and down the paths between the vines, stopping to greet people at other tables, talking for a moment about this and that, all the women taking a turn to lay a hand on the new roundness of my *pancettina.*

'Her arm encircling my waist, Maria-Luce and I walked up to the second terrace and then the third. Higher up on that moonstruck ridge, we could hear the groaning of the sea. We looked down upon the vines, even and straight like fine green stitching upon rough red-brown cloth, watched the torches leaping in the dark, primitive dancers evoking the gods and keeping time to the melody of muffled voices, the *bocce* clicking along the packed earth and the steady strum of a mandolin. We stood there quietly until—and I don't recall who started it—we began to laugh, to throw our heads back and laugh ourselves to tears.

'Dabbing her eyes with a balled-up handkerchief, she then put it back in her pocket, took it out again, trying to find words. Knowing she was trying but not knowing which words she was searching for, I couldn't help her. Still looking down upon the *festa,* she said, "Like a *pastello.* All the lines smudged. No hard edges. Everything and everyone is more beautiful from a distance. But it's up close to one another that we mostly live our lives. Antonia, I pray you'll always be happy here. That you'll stay."

'It seemed a strange thing to say, the part about *hoping* that I'd stay. I told her, "Of course I'll stay."

'"I always wished for daughters. Much as I adore my sons. But you know it's female to female, mother to daughter, that's how what matters most is passed down. It wasn't my destiny to have daughters but it will be yours." She touched my belly, held her hand there. "You're carrying a girl, Antonia. It's a baby girl you've made, I'm sure of it. And you'll have others. And they will. How many generations could your mother count back, do you know?"

'"Two is all she ever talked about. Her mother, her grandmother. But counting her and counting me, that makes four. Yes, four."

'"Good. Yes, that's fine," Maria-Luce said. "And so now you, you and what's been passed on to you from that line, have come to live here. Like a ewe who was shepherded to graze with a new flock, you may feel out of place from time to time. I mean, life takes twists and turns. You know that. Nevertheless, the truth is that this land, this place is yours now. Yours to pass on. And I know it will be through daughters. Oh, I'm not forgetting Ugo, not at all. But he'll never marry. He has no concern for what or who will come after him, it's only the *now* that interests him: the hunt, his automobiles, his travels. Unlike ewes, rams stray. They're able to manage anywhere. That leaves you. And Tancredi of course. But I'm so very happy that you're here. That it's you, *proprio tu*, exactly you, who will carry on."

'Of course she knew. Sure as a seer could, Maria-Luce knew.

'It was only a day and its night that he'd been ill. The fever rose and never broke. Three days after the second anniversary of our marriage and just a month or so before Filippa would be a year old, Tancredi died. It wanted time for me to forgive Maria-Luce for banning me from our room. From my husband. Fearful Tancredi would infect me, and I Filippa, through my milk, it was she who sat with him, bathed him, spoke to him. I could hear her singing to him as I stood outside the door. It was she who closed his eyes, lit the candles. Washed him in oil warmed over the flames.

'The funeral smell still in the house, it was less than a week later that Maria-Luce died. A broken heart or the diphtheria, no one knew for sure which took her. And so we were four: Battista, Ugo, Filippa and I, each of us grown-ups grieving in a private way. It was Battista who asked Marco-Tullio to come and stay at the villa, to do what he could to comfort Filippa and me. I hardly noticed any of them. Not even Filippa. During those first days and nights I would hold her to my breast when she cried but it was Marco-Tullio who cared for her, murmuring lullabies and feeding her bits of sweet things, honey from a small, square gelato spoon. With her tucked in his arms, he would read to her, looking down, now and then, at her upturned eyes, enchanting her. Much the same way he had once enchanted me. I remember that.

'Soon enough Ugo began his travels again and I the mothering of my little girl, thus leaving Marco-Tullio and Battista to wander about the land, busying them-selves—or pretending to—with the operations of the farm. Their women gone, they grew beards, avoided washing themselves or parting with their linen. More about their lives could be read from the stains on their shirts and the furrows in their foreheads than from anything they might venture to say. On evenings that were fine, one of them would carry Filippa's cradle out onto the veranda. They'd pull up chairs on either side of it and sit there, each one rocking it with the toe of a boot. A bowl of fruit on a table nearby, they'd peel and slice and eat from the points of their knives and when one of them found a piece particularly sweet and juicy, he'd cut it in two, offer half to Filippa if she wasn't already asleep. Though Marco-Tullio was eleven years Battista's junior, the only striking difference between them was the quality of their boots: my father's, biannual hand-mades from the *ciabattino* in Pontremoli; Battista's, black Hermès riding boots with deep whisky-coloured cuffs. Mornings, afternoons, hands locked behind their backs, stories locked inside their boys' hearts, the two widowers walked and smoked. A man's kind of grieving. Neither having loved well nor been well loved, I wondered if they grieved at all. When one has not loved or been loved, what is it that one feels if not grief? And I wondered, too, about their boots. How much can be told about a man from his boots.'

Antonia stops, looks at me. 'Marlena, I don't think I've told you how my father died, have I? Marco-Tullio was shot twice in the chest by a *repubblichino*. Do you know what a *repubblichino* was?'

'A Fascist true to Mussolini's Salò.'

'*Brava*. Not sufficient that Italians and Germans and Allies were killing one another, Italians killed Italians. Civil war within the Occupation. Well, twice a week or so, Marco-Tullio would set off with a foraging sack filled with bread and eggs and whatever else could be found, cart the goods up to the *branchi* in the mountains, the bands of Partigiani living in the caves. When one of the Partigiani brought my father back to the villa, we found *I Promessi Sposi* buttoned inside his shirt, one of the bullets having pierced it. I miss my father.'

She waits. 'That was late in 1943. I've gone ahead too far. I will return to the winter of 1940.

'It gave way early to spring and, at table each day, Marco-Tullio spoke of getting back to his farm. Knowing well that he couldn't stay, I said nothing to convince him otherwise though I felt moved to pack up my baby and go home with him. To be a little away from Tancredi or to get closer to him, I didn't know which. But Maria-Luce spoke up then, saying in my ear what she'd told me on that evening up on the ridge. *Like a ewe who was shepherded to graze with a new flock or a lamb who strayed, you may feel out of place from time to time. Life takes twists and turns. You know that.*

'I did know that. I had come to know it better. Twists and turns. When I announced my plans, it was Ugo, just returned, who quietly told me no. Battista and Marco-Tullio echoing him, Ugo had another plan. Marco-Tullio's farm was small enough that the *fattore* at Castelletto could find hands to keep it going. Too, the farm was close enough by that Marco-Tullio could oversee certain of the work himself. Everything could be arranged. My father would live with us at Castelletto.'

Antonia stops, looks about, surprised somehow that we are all sitting there so close to her. Timidly, she looks down, the bridal glow spent. As though eavesdropping on her own memories, she flinches, water welling in her eyes, shimmering, never falling. Rising from her chair, she walks to where Luce sits, leans down a bit over her, ruffles her hair, softly pulls a handful of it, tilting her daughter's face up to hers. They smile at each other. Antonia walks away from us. Her hair loosed from its pins and tumbled to her waist, from behind she is a lissom girl in a long brown dress. Over her shoulder, she says,

'*Sogni d'oro pulcini. A domani.* Golden dreams, little chicks. Until tomorrow.'

After that particular evening, the gathering-together to cook, the post-supper storytelling takes on another tenor. On the face of things nothing much changes. The room quietens, Antonia begins. But her linear, era-by-era telling she trades for spontaneous recall. This leads the others to do the same. One of the daughters asks a question and three will answer it while another is already asking the next question, until they are mostly talking to one another while Antonia listens. Sitting stirring cognac into her gold-rimmed, footed porcelain cup, one can see that the shift from her soliloquy to their *allegria* is what she intends. After an evening or two, the thread of Antonia's story seems forgotten. Surely it has been broken.

She saves the pieces though, marks her place. It is on our mornings together that she continues.

'It was not quite a year after Tancredi's death—I remember it was cool and so surely it was autumn—when it occurred to me that I was being appraised. *Looked at* with intent. By Battista, by Ugo. More than once during those months, Marco-Tullio had broached the subject of my marrying Ugo, saying it was the common thing to do—a man to wed his brother's widow. As from far away, I could hear my father speaking to me but I couldn't answer him. I didn't care to answer him. My eyes squeezed nearly shut, I didn't care to wake from the half-dream where I'd gone to live with Tancredi, where I could still hear him, still smell him. Still be with him. How easy it was to call him up at will. *Ah, there he is. Hair a sheet of shined copper, eyes the colour of a shallow sea, he pushes open the kitchen door, stands still for a moment. Two long strides and he's next to me. Shaking his head and smiling, drawing me to him, cupping my buttocks in his big beautiful hands, he whispers to me. Together we go to Filippa then, to her cradle near the fire. Sleeping or not, he takes her from the nest of coverlets, holds her high, croons to her, kisses her, how in love is Tancredi with his baby girl.*

'Tancredi a ghost between us, Ugo and I married in the spring of 1941. I'd thought then it was me who'd invited Tancredi to be wherever we were, to walk where we did, to breathe and eat and sleep and make love with us. It was much later that I began to understand it was Ugo who'd kept his brother near. You see, Ugo feared me.

I know that sounds strange, but he did and it wanted a war and its malice before I came to understand that. He feared *loving* me and so, with Tancredi present, he might indulge that fear. Forbid love. It worked for a time.

'There being no love—no man–woman love—between us, Ugo and I were free to enjoy each other. He had his books and his guns and his automobiles, his journeys here and there. I had Filippa. It was not as though we lived separately: he followed the daily sagas of the farm, of Marco-Tullio and Battista. He was a benevolent father to Filippa. And to me he was good, gentle, generous. As I consider it, my early marriage to Ugo was ideal, in its way.

'We made our private quarters up in the *mansarda*, up there where the Castelletto men have their place now. Ugo had an ornate yellow porcelain wood stove installed up under the eaves, a thing more Austrian or Russian than Tuscan, and we spent our evenings playing with Filippa, reading to her and then to each other. We argued more about events in books than those of our lives, using someone else's words in lieu of our own when we had hard things to say. Tancredi sat between us. Not wishing to assign him the status of god by avoiding his name, Ugo talked about Tancredi as though he was in the next room. Kept his ghost close by. How easy it is to love the dead.

'I don't think Ugo had other women but I was never certain. A truth long past knowing, still I wonder. What I do know is that, as much as we were together, I was no rival to Ugo's solitude. Or to time with his friends. Always more frequent and unexplained were his journeys and, when he was here, he hunted with old mates, drank and schemed and shouted with them long into many nights up there under the eaves. They spoke of the war. Always the war. Roaring anti-Fascists, were Ugo and his mates. Of the purest, deepest red. Toscana has always been red. It was when Battista joined the men that they entered into the most hellish arguments. Red enough himself, Battista managed to find voice to praise Mussolini, the Mussolini of the twenties and early thirties, for his programs activated before *suo auto-intossicazione*, his self-intoxication. Battista reminded Ugo that state funds distributed by Il Duce's *bonifica integrale* made it possible for landowners such as himself to restore and reclaim unusable land, to build roads, lay irrigation pipes. To restore the sharecroppers' housing to decency. *Do you think I could have afforded to keep nine farmhouses in good condition without that aid? What was gifted to us we passed on to our farmers, relieving a very old misery. Shall we forget that? Quiet. Stay quiet, Ugo,* Battista would tell him.

'He listened to his father. Never putting his name to the official Fascist agreement, neither did Ugo flaunt dissent. Unspoken defiance might keep the sneering Blackshirt bullies at bay. A man might avoid extradition and beatings. Torture. Ugo did. Understanding that every time he drove into the village, rode up onto the high meadows, settled into the barber's chair for a shave, paced the veranda with a midnight cigar, the ground could give way. Somewhere inside me I might have understood that, too. I think I did.

'And while the men did their talking, Filippa and I were tucked in our warm feather bed behind the door. We had our own things to talk about, Filippa and I, and then we'd sleep some, awaken when the men's voices broke through our tranquillity. Mostly I suppose we waited for Ugo.

'Finally spent, when the others had gone on their way, Ugo would open the door, stand there looking at us, grinning in the light of a guttering candle.

'Filippa would sit up. "*Ciao, papà.*"

'"*Ciao,* Filippetta."

'He'd undress, climb in on the other side of Filippa, embrace her, leaving his hand free to hold mine above her little head, and that's often how we fell asleep.

'But the talk up in the *mansarda* and in our dining room was at odds with what one heard in the village or broadcast on the radio, read in the newspapers, most all of which reported the cheering of the Italian population entire over our entry into the war. Echoing Mussolini, there was a haughtiness, a cocksure stance about the people. Il Duce would never have dragged his less-than-prepared and -outfitted troops into a war in which victory was less than certain and quick. A few weeks of war, a pittance to pay for a share in Hitler's spoils. After that Sunday in December of 1941, insolence cooled, hardened into something like bravado. I pushed all of it out of mind. One could do that then.

'Towards the end of 1942, news of British and American bombardment of Italian cities became commonplace. Buildings destroyed, people killed; I knew the numbers but I hid from them. The RAF bombarded Torino, Milano and Genova in October; days later the Americans struck Genova again, Milano again. Genova—its strategic position on the coast less than a hundred kilometres from Castelletto—again. Again. Six times in all Genova was hit by December. Still I could banish the war. Make it a faraway thing, an opera playing in another town, the vainglorious pig screaming *Vincere, vincere, e vinceremo* through his pouting puppet's lips, the tragicomic star. It would all soon be over. Surely it would. The Germans were winning, France had capitulated, England was being massacred. No time at all and *tutto fatto*. All over.

'Just the same, we began to enlarge our stores. To keep all we had, to sell nothing. The farmers did the same with their shares of flour and maize and olive oil and wine. Wool from the sheep. Together we dried fruits and vegetables, poached and canned them, made jams, butchered more animals than we needed, set the meat to dry in one form or another. Working alongside the farmers, there were times when it seemed we were preparing for some local *festa* or putting up food for a longer, harder winter than usual. More tribute to illusion. I think there were some who'd already bowed to the Fates, though, understanding that what would be had already been written. I envied them. I still do. Let the Fates take the blame. Better they than us.

'I really don't know how much more I care to say about the war. Everyone has either lived it or heard about it, read about it, looked at it, its truths familiar. Over six years, fifty-five million people died for the delirious vanity of three men. That's the juice. Isn't that the juice? Damn them. Damn the Fates. Damn their inextinguishable noise.'

CHAPTER IX

Days pass, maybe three or four, and the troupe meets at sunset, when we cook and dine together. As far as I know, no one has asked Antonia why she's interrupted her story.

A glass of wine in each hand, Luce invites me to smoke with her out on the veranda one evening, and we go to settle on the stone wall and look out over the olive grove. Not until our cigarettes are half smoked does she say, 'I want to be sure that you're not thinking that Antonia has withdrawn from her storytelling because of you.'

'No, I've not been thinking that.' I want to tell her that her mother has not withdrawn her storytelling but rather that she continues it when we walk together in the morning. I'm torn. If I say this to Luce, will I be breaking a trust with Antonia? If I don't tell her, I am being false. Or can I call my reticence another of those sins of omission?

Luce continues, 'Good. Filippa and I and some of the others, we thought you might have felt that she couldn't proceed because you're . . . you know, you're . . .'

'Not one of you?'

'Something like that. I think the opposite is true. That she can't go on while the rest of us are present.'

'Well, actually I . . .'

'You see, Marlena, even Filippa and I, we don't know the rest of the story. And what we do know, well, it didn't come from Antonia but from Filippa's memories. From a four-year-old's, a five-year-old's glimpses, shadows. All I know comes from Filippa. It was when Viola and Isotta were still babies and Sabina an infant, when we were all camping out in my flat in Bologna while I was at university, it was then that Filippa told me what she remembered. What haunted her. Haunts her. *Soldier is hurting Mamma. Mamma screaming. Mamma crying. Soldier is hurting me. Can't breathe, can't see. I hear Mamma screaming.*

I try to scream but I can't. Everything is dark but I can hear. I hear a big sound, a crash, a man laughing. Another crash, the man laughing. Mamma, why don't you help me?

'Was Mamma violated by the Germans? Was Filippa? It's almost *expected*, isn't it? Conquerors rape the women of the conquered. Often their children. Hasn't that always been the case? I never knew the women who lived here with Mamma during the war. Families were scattered by the time I was growing up. Laws changed, the *mezzadria* discarded, some of the farmers stayed on as day workers but those who could went to work in the villages, the cities. It's likely that Giorgia knows something. Biagio does. He was thirteen, fourteen, fifteen during the war. What he knows, he'll take to the tomb. Battista, my father's father . . . perhaps he knew what happened, but his Tuscan reserve was inviolate as Biagio's. There are others who know, or think they do. Tales, speculation, invention passed on like gospel. Like the remedy for a viper bite. But not to us. Never to us. The only part of the war that Mamma has talked about from time to time are her romantic notions of the days when all the women and the old men and the children lived together here in the villa while the men were off fighting or in work camps in Germany or, when the Resistenza rose up, camped in the hill caves. Mamma's heart is Tuscan red and I think she must have been in her glory, the young matriarch seeing to the common good. Some may have had affection for her during that epoch of need but I suspect the greater, more enduring emotion felt for the farmer's daughter who married out of her class into the family of *il padrono* was envy. The sort of envy which survives the generations. People still stop talking sometimes when Filippa or Antonia or I enter the bar, the doctor's waiting room, the church.'

'And you and Filippa, you've never spoken to your own daughters about . . . ?'

'What, really, has there been to say? I think our daughters have spoken among themselves, wondered together, but their lives have always remained remote from those events. The vacancies in the de Gaspari history are nothing more than that . . . empty spaces. Every family has them. And then came Magda.

'She was ten, perhaps younger, when she began to plague Isotta for stories about the Belgian who fathered her. While she was at it, she worked on Antonia. *Tell me, Nonnina. Tell me about* . . . Sweet as she is, also is she more *demanding* than are the rest of us. Magda confronts Antonia. And Antonia refuses to be confronted. They are alike. They seem almost the same person to us. The young Antonia, the aged Antonia. The stand-off endures.

'If my father were still alive, if he . . . oh, it's not as though I never tried to speak with him about the war. I was still a little girl when I began begging him to tell me the stories: what happened to him when he and Mamma were separated, what happened here, what happened to Mamma and Filippa. Such pain would invade his eyes, such desolation, it was I who would tell him, "*Va bene, papà, lasciamo stare.* It's okay, we'll leave it be."

'You see, I think we could help her, that we could comfort Mamma if she would only allow it. If it's shame or guilt or some such burden she carries, we, Filippa and I, could help her. It's not that we, any of us save Magda, need to know for ourselves—it's not that at all. It's Mamma's consolation we want.'

I have never heard Luce call Antonia 'Mamma' before this evening. Hearing her say that word changes things for me. I don't understand why or how. It doesn't matter. I ask her for another cigarette. She lights one, hands it to me, lights one for herself. I say, 'And you, when you've asked Antonia, asked your mother to . . . ?'

'Mamma's pact of silence is with herself. Irrevocable. Or so it seemed. Filippa and I believe that Antonia will likely continue her story with you. We can see, we *feel* she would like that. Magda agrees. We understand she can't face telling us together or one of us alone . . . We think—hope—that she *will* tell you and once she has, it might be easier for her to tell us. I am not asking you to betray her confidence—nothing like that. That you *aren't* a family member . . . what I mean is that Antonia's sentiments for you are *instinctive*, just as I think yours are for her. You are drawn to each other in the same way. After all, what do either of you really *know*, one about the other? And yet . . .'

'What do you want me to do?'

'To listen to her.'

Let life shape itself.

CHAPTER X

'Here's a great dish for you, a kind of Tuscan stone soup. During the war it was festival food. *Pizzicotti.* Bread dough, half-risen, herbs, a pot of boiling water. When we ran out of flour, we used chestnut flour; when we ran out of chestnut flour, we made *acquacotta*, or a version of it. Water, wild sage, sometimes there was a cabbage or an egg. Sit down and help me, will you?'

When she wasn't waiting for me on the white road this morning, I thought Antonia had gone on ahead. Not finding her on the high meadow or in the pine wood, I followed the path down to the sea but there was no one.

Antonia had stayed abed for once, I told myself, knowing it wasn't true. I gathered cones for the fire and walked among the rocks. The skin of the sea taut and blue as a length of stretched silk, where was Antonia?

I worked, packed up for the day, bathed and rested. No sign of Biagio or any of the others. I wondered if I should or shouldn't go up to the villa. It was after five when I took a shawl and climbed the road, found her alone in the kitchen sitting in front of a small mound of dough, pinching off pieces of it, rolling and stretching each one into an oval the size of a small olive.

'I've been expecting you.'

'I thought you might be . . . Were you not feeling well this morning?'

'Something like that. I got as far as the veranda and . . . well, disinclined as I am to admit it, I was *tired*. My legs heavy as a dead man's. I just sat down and stayed there rocking until the light came. I thought to send one of them down to tell you, to take the thermos to you, but by the time they stirred, well, I knew you'd already be . . . I drank it all myself.'

'No, no. No need to . . . I missed you, though.'

'Was there much to pick?'

'I can't say I really noticed.'

'Will you finish these while I get to the lamb? Luce and Filippa have taken Sabina to Firenze for a few days, Viola is dining in Carrara with journalists from Roma, and Magda has gone with Giangiacomo to visit his parents. I haven't seen or heard from Isa, though I know she's off somewhere since her boots are gone. I can tell who's here, who's not by what boots are waiting by the kitchen door. Mostly I can tell that way but not always. As for supper this evening, I think we'll be only four. Biagio, Giorgia and you and me, since I understand that Umberto has made off with Fernando. A most *intimate* gathering. I was hoping it would be fine enough to set up on the veranda? What do you think about—'

'You seem so sad.'

'Can you wait for tea until I fix the lamb?' Addressing her words in the direction of where I stand, Antonia has not yet looked at me. Busying herself at another part of the table, she asks, 'Do you know what I long for sometimes? To dine alone. To fix a dish or two that please me, to set out my preferred plates and things on a small table by the fire, light candles, pour wine; I don't know if I would like music, perhaps only the sounds of the fire, of whatever birds and beasts are flitting about outdoors. I think that would be enough. Before Fernando came to join you, I often thought about you and your little solitary meals down there in the lodge and I'd envy you. I'm sure one of the reasons I stay awake half the night is so I can be alone. Awake and alone. And my morning walks are an extension of the night. *The beauty of solitude*, I think we've talked about that.'

'We've also talked about growing so used to people that it's not until they're gone that we begin to miss them. Something like that.'

'I'm not wishing anyone away for more than a respite. Now and then. Brief, mostly; not so brief, sometimes.'

Antonia is slicing the flesh from a shoulder of lamb, mincing it finely, placing it in a large white bowl, adding a pan of breadcrumbs which she's just taken from the oven. Stoning dried olives, crushing purple-skinned garlic, mincing rosemary, she mixes all these together in the white bowl with the lamb and the bread, adds a beaten egg, a long pour of white wine, sea salt. Now she rubs more sea salt over two tiny haunches of suckling lamb, then pats the mixture thickly over them, one side only. From a basket on the floor she pulls branches of wild rosemary, wets them with oil, lays them whole in a shallow terracotta dish, places the legs of lamb over them, tucking the branches nicely underneath the flesh so they'll flavour it but won't burn. She covers the dish with a white cloth.

'I've lit the oven on the veranda so it should be ready by eight. In any case I won't put these in until everyone's here. They'll need an hour at most, I would think. Maybe less, plump little things.'

Still avoiding my eyes, she washes her hands, rinses them a long time under the tap, takes another white cloth from the endless stacks of them in the drawers of an old dresser. Meanwhile I've nearly exhausted the dough, rolling and stretching it the way she'd done.

'You'll need to flour those, lay them in a single layer on that tray.' As she points to the tray which is behind me, she looks at me. She looks for a long time. 'Do you recall my telling you about my game?'

'Game? I don't think . . .'

'My pretending that every day is my last. That game. *Nothing squandered or cloaked.* Sometimes it doesn't seem quite enough that I've told myself the truth. That *longing* I've tried to explain, part of it may be a wish to tell some truths to others. I'll begin with you. I'm angry with you, violently so. I had every intention this morning to ask you to quit my property—Biagio's old place being more mine than his—to leave it and us and never to return. It was anger that weakened my legs, left me fixed to my chair, an enfeebled old dame. I . . .'

She is saying more but the red whirring in my ears is louder than she, a fierce wind pushing through a narrow reed, and, unlike the evening of her first cannonade, the words I've already heard strike and pierce. On the heels of inviting me to supper, she's throwing me out . . . I want to run but now it's my own legs, *heavy as a dead man's*. The scream inside me escapes as a whisper. 'Why? What . . . ?'

'Because you've stirred it all up around here, foisted yourself upon us, you and your—'

'My what? Please, tell me.'

But she's already turned away. Half away, her face in profile, a violet flush on her cheek. I step closer but she raises a hand to stop me. Her shoulders heave in a gentle rhythm and tears pool upon the brown wool of her bosom. 'Sins of omission. I'm leaving a string of them, a lifetime of them and somehow you have—what is it that you've done?—*awakened* me to the gravity of those omissions.

Tu e i tuoi occhi che fanno pensá. You and your eyes that make one think.'

I sit down, trace a circle in the flour on the board, stay quiet until my breath grows even.

'I think you're mistaken, *signora*,' I say at last. 'Not my eyes but those six pairs of blue ones, it's those that cause you *to think*.'

Face drenched, tiny points of blue diamonds glistening from eyes screwed nearly shut, she turns to me. 'Will you go to walk with me up to the high meadow? Will you sit with me for a while in the grass?'

I shake my head, *no*.

CHAPTER XI

I am sorry for this old woman's pain but sorry, too, that I'd once again stood still while she flung her rope about the scapegoat me. Wordless, bewildered, I take my shawl, turn away from her, walk back down the white road.

I throw Fernando's and my things into two valises, stuff what won't fit into string shopping bags and place it all outside the door. I strip the princess bed, fold the linens, tidy the already tidy space, write a simple non-indicting note to Biagio, and sit out on the step to wait for Fernando even though I know he's gone to Carrara with Umberto, that they plan to attend a meeting of the

Tourist Development Association there, of which Umberto is president, that they will join some of his colleagues for dinner afterwards. I'm too mad to lie one last time on the princess bed though I feel tired and maybe a little sick. I clean the flour from under my fingernails. I hear her then. The *enfeebled old dame* gone away, it is an imperious Antonia who strides towards the lodge. I neither acknowledge her approach nor move from my place, and it's she who comes to sit next to me.

'We're acting like mother and daughter, you know,' she tells me.

'You're playing both roles.'

'Perhaps that's true.' She looks at the readied baggage. 'It may help you to know that I also told Filippa and Luce and Sabina—the only three whom I've seen today—to leave as well. They pay no attention to me. I wish you wouldn't.'

'I'm doing one better than that.'

'By taking me at my word?'

'Being old, being troubled, neither one is licence to behave the madwoman.'

'You may continue to believe that for another decade or two.'

A scant six centimetres of cement between us on the narrow step, I can smell thyme and mint on her clothes, her breath. From the tail of my eye, I see there is flour under her fingernails, too. She's looking at me but I don't turn to her.

'I shall be sorry to lose you,' she says.

Without wanting to, my reflex is to turn fast to face her. To confront her. 'Why do you stare? What are you looking for in me?' I want to know.

'Myself. Another view of myself. I think that's what it is. And you, what are you looking for in me? A glimpse of the old woman you'll become? You *have* noted the similarities in us, have you not? Oh, our form is different, I grant you, but as for the rest, well . . . since that first evening when you came to dinner, both of us knew we were the same. I'd found my sparring partner in you and so got right down to the fight. Or tried to. I trusted you to understand and you did. That was why you let me go on, wasn't it? I'm not saying we agreed then or since then about *particulars*. I've lived another life. *Ma è come siamo fatti*—it's how we're *made* that's the same. Our *inwardness*. I know why you can't be hurt, why I couldn't raise more than a squeak out of you that night around the table . . . it's because you've already lived through the greatest pain of your life and so there's nothing left that can make you tear out your hair, gnash your teeth. And that's why you say you're *full*, that you can be well anywhere . . . Am I getting warm?'

Looking down, I say, 'Maybe a little warm.'

'*Complimenti.* My compliments. You wear pain as skilfully as you paint your lovely red mouth. You, whoever you are— and by the way, I don't know and don't need to know—you and I, we're connected in a way that exceeds blood. I think it's rare. It may not be, but I, myself, have never known it before. It's why I can be brutal to you in the way I am to myself. And why I can love you as I want so much to love myself. Yes, here I am telling you that *I love you*.'

I look straight ahead now, fumbling for her hand, and she helps me, folds hers into mine and we sit there on the step. The light's gone blue, a darkish blue, the dusky bloom on a damson plum. The blue just before twilight.

'And as for being loved, your Byzantine is *besotted*.'

'We both are. When one of us isn't being horrid.'

'I say you're good together. Somehow Fernando reminds me of Ugo. He's weak the way Ugo was and strong the way he was. Will you give him a chance to scale the walls to *save his princess*? He can do it, you know.'

'I do know. But I'm still working on climbing his. Everything in its time. Walls scaled, walls untried . . . by chance, by searching, more by blundering we've managed to find so many little doors in our walls, secret doors into the places behind them. We are good together.'

She's left her hand curled into mine and all of a sudden I notice how little it weighs there. After a while she looks at me and, still holding my hand, pulls me up from the step. 'Come now, fix me a parting tea.'

She sets out the tea things while I put the kettle on, light some candles.

'Do you recall about where I left off my story?'

I don't answer her though I recall exactly. I pour water, hissing, into the teapot and it splatters on my hand. I suck the burn, say, '*Over six years, fifty-five million people died for the delirious vanity of three men.* It was there. A rather memorable line.'

'Yes, well, as it happened, Vittorio Emanuele III signed us out of Germany's war in 1943, sent little Benito off to the Abruzzo. But even as the steeple bells were hurling chimes of victory through the warm, grape-smelling September air, the next war had begun. The next three wars, to be precise. Having staged a cinematically daring airborne raid on Campo Imperatore and rescuing Mussolini two days after the King had confined him there, Hitler then set him up in the puppet republic at Salò. The homecoming Italian soldiers who remained true to Mussolini—the *repubblichini*—continued to fight the Allies with the Germans. Too, the *repubblichini* took on another enemy, those other homecoming Italian soldiers, the ones who wanted nothing more of Fascism or Mussolini or Hitler's war and so hid themselves in the woods and the mountains all over the peninsula. The *imboscati*, they were called, "the ones hidden among the trees". So we had war between Fascists and Allies. Another between Fascist Italians and non-Fascist Italians. That makes two wars. And soon enough la Resistenza reared up, making war number three. Composed of yet other homecoming soldiers plus those boys who'd been too young to fight, and men—such as Ugo and Battista and Marco-Tullio—who'd been too old to fight, plus more than fifty thousand women, all of them wanting nothing more of Mussolini or the Germans. Or the Italians who did. La Resistenza's war was with the Germans—lately pals, now Occupiers—as well as with the *repubblichini*. And the grand Allies? The same ones who'd strafed and bombed and maimed Italy until hours before the armistice was signed? *Voilà*, they became our *new* pals. *Saviours* they were called, though not by the already motherless children or the childless mothers. No, not by them.

'The threat of a German presence at Castelletto now probable, Ugo and the men who remained on the farms set to work to prepare for it. Like vigilantes they were, riding out to the far confines of the property to each of the nine *casolari*, helping the families—women, old men, children—to pack clothes, bedding, food, eventually to load them and their goods into tractor-pulled wagons. It wanted weeks, two, perhaps three, to gather everyone together in the villa.

'With the help of Abriana and Tessa I'd already begun to transform the villa into a communal house. Nearing fifteen by then, still small as a child, her legs thin as a new foal's, Tessa shadowed her mother and me, anticipating the next task and the next, porting baskets of wet laundry on her head, heaving the heavy dripping sheets over the line, polishing the endless stretches of red tiles on her hands and knees. I'd sometimes stop to watch her . . . her delicate child's form with a strapping woman's strength . . . and think again and again about what Maria-Luce had told me long ago when I posed a question to her about Abri's husband—Tessa's father. Who was he?

"'Only Abri knows," she'd said. "When she told me she was with child and, weeping like a banshee, begged me to keep her and to allow the child to live here too, I said of course I would. You see, Abri's parents were third-generation sharecroppers at Castelletto and already had six, maybe seven children by the time Abri was born. Too poor to keep another baby, when she was a few months old, Abri's mother brought her to the kitchen door tucked nicely inside a wooden crate which smelled of ripe quince. Abri has never lived anywhere else but here. Though we thought to raise her as a daughter and did so for years, she slowly slipped into the ways of a servant, saying she liked it best that way. And so it seemed natural enough that she would bear her child and that it, too, would become part of this family. There was never any question of her returning to her real kin. I never asked Abri about her lover, not feeling the need to know and she never feeling the need to tell."

'When Maria-Luce died, Abri moved herself and her little girl from their pale yellow room on the second floor where they always lived to the two tiny ones next to the wash house. I don't think Abri ever stopped mourning for her mistress. Her mother, really.

'And so there we were, Abri, Tessa and I heaving ancient furnishings into storerooms, setting up make-shift beds scavenged from attics and cellars; we created dormitories of a kind, one for babies and their mothers, one for children and the women who would watch over them, one for older women who were ill. For men and boys, we set up sleeping rooms in the nearby wood sheds and summer kitchens. Three families refused to leave their homes on the outlying lands, preferring isolation to community, and so our household during the early days of the Occupation counted thirty-eight souls, including Battista, Marco-Tullio, Filippa and me, and for a while, Ugo. Fifteen women, four babies, eleven older children, Biagino among them, eight men. Once everyone had a place to sleep, we began burying food. In unlikely places we dug deep ditches, lined them with leaves and branches, laid down haunches of prosciutto, wheels of pecorini, strings of dried sausages, whole *finocchione*, all of them looking like so many little corpses shrouded in winding cloths. Prophetic images.

'We rationed our stores, organised cooking and baking and mealtimes, rotated turns in the wash house, spun wool, sewed and knitted and mended; even bathing times were posted. Much as it had since the young men went off to fight at the end of 1940, the work in the fields proceeded. We harvested the grapes, made the wine, brought in the wheat, picked the apples, the pears, the quince, the figs, the olives. Fear was soothed by endless tasks. Each of us was mother or father to all the children, each of us wanted the others' tranquillity and thus found his own. It was a primitive life, reduced—or was it elevated?—to the fundamentals of food, shelter, affection, and for those months we lived in something close to harmony. Closer to it than I have ever lived before or since. Everything we did was aimed at the wolf, at keeping him from the door. The wolf that was hunger, the wolf that was all the hungers. I've always been sorry that my girls and theirs have never lived that elementally. That *critically*. Filippa was four when it began and her memories are limited to flashes, fragments, by reason of age or selectivity, I'm not certain which. In the here and now, my girls have too much. Once the war was over, Filippa had too much. Luce always has. The rest of them, too. Even so they've done well, mostly avoiding the perils of abundance, of paths already carved, of inherited lives. Still I wonder who they might have become had they grown up straddling that rousing place between sufficiency and want where you feel your supper right down to your toes. I'm convinced that's the best place. You hit what I'd thought to be a long-dead nerve that first morning up on the *alto piano*. You see, I *am* one of those whose best days were lived during a war. Best days. Worst days, too.

'Since the events of September, Ugo had been making forays up into the hills, staying away for days, sometimes longer, but it was in November 1943 when Ugo left Castelletto, telling me he'd be a longer time away. *I think it will be months, Antonia. It could be months.* Setting out in one of the farm trucks loaded with food and clothes, rifles, pistols—and yes, a pair of Bredas wrapped in blankets—he never said much in the way of goodbye, only that he was off to take his turn to fight, to hole further up in the mountains where bands of the Resistenza were forming. Laughing in his rueful way, he said he would be the *old man* among them, their Cerberus. And from time to time, he was. But he did more than that. Though I never understood it at the time, Ugo had been sharpening his claws for years. The skulking behaviour, the undisclosed journeys, the meetings in the village and up in the *mansarda*; you see, Ugo had long been moving in the clandestine whorls of the OSS, the Office of Strategic Services. The American intelligence organisation. He raised funds—principally his own—trafficked arms, established underground presses, collaborated in the masterminding of train derailings, bombings, kidnappings, assassinations. Propaganda, espionage, subversion, sabotage: *caro* Ugo was a gentleman spy. Saying brief and unsentimental farewells to Battista, Marco-Tullio, even more token ones to the rest of the household, he held me in his arms, rocked me there for a while. And then he was gone. I stood on the veranda watching the wretched truck sputtering down the oak road and out of sight, thinking he'd been wise, Ugo had, staying with me until the rhythms of the full house had taken hold, until the new pace of things had strengthened me. He knew I'd be well. And because he knew I would be, I was.

Now and then Maria-Luce gave a hand, whispering, *I'm so happy that you're here. That it's you,* proprio tu, *exactly you, who will carry on.*

'It was then, at the end of November 1943, when news came that the Germans had requisitioned farms and moved into villages close enough to us to thin our illusions that they would pass us by. Though days and nights followed the same pattern, we began to *expect* them, the Huns. As in a death watch, we waited.

'Rumbling up the oak walk in trucks and motorcycles and two long black automobiles, even on horseback, Wehrmacht Huns marched into Castelletto on the first of December 1943, just before seven in the morning. One of those dates and times one remembers. I was standing on the veranda, holding Filippa by the hand. A welcoming committee of two. From the shouting, the dust, the screeching of flapping hens in one of the trucks, a group tramped up the steps to where we stood. One of them—though I knew nothing then of rank, I would later learn he was a colonel—asked to see the woman of the house. *La padrona*, he said, his voice sounding like those men in the films, boxers who've had their teeth punched out and try to speak through a mouthful of blood. That's how he sounded to me. It's how they all sounded. That impression remains. Even now, when I hear a German speak I hear it through a mouthful of blood. Setting off a round of lewd looks and grunts, I told him, *Sono io, la padrona*. I am the patroness.

'Another early impression which has never left me is that German men have feminine lips, turgid, sensual, and that they move them as women do, this being only one of the traits that accentuate their perversity. Neither men nor women, they are some race of satyr. In any case, the colonel informed me that nine officers would be living in the villa. The others—I don't know, I think there must have been thirty or more, but the number changed all the time, some leaving, others arriving—would camp in the outbuildings or in tents.

'The officers chose their quarters among the upstairs rooms and the *mansarda* and their lackeys came to move out beds and furniture which did not suit them, peruse the house for what did: paintings, the baby grand, a sixteenth-century wall-size mirror, Turkey carpets, towels, linens, even Battista's dressing-gown. All the farmers' belongings from the dormitories were thrown in a heap out onto the wet gravel road. An aide to the colonel announced to me that everyone who'd been living in the villa was to be relocated by sunset. Anyone still "loitering" in the house or on the grounds after that would be shot.

'Those who were not already out in the fields when the Huns arrived set about rummaging the heap for their things. Tying them up in blankets, lifting the bundles onto their backs, their heads, they trekked back to their farms. But what they found of their old homes, their patches of land, was only devastation. The Huns had stopped to strip the fields and gardens, clear out what pittance was left in the cellars and storerooms, to rape the few women they could find, burn the houses and barns, slaughter the animals. And a boy of eleven who raised a rifle to them. The Huns had warmed up on their way to us. Homeless, starving, with no destination save to outwit them for another day, a few more hours, these refugees moved through woods, along hunters' trails, found succour in the caves of the Partigiani and in the mountain huts of shepherds. Theirs are the stories you should tell.

'The only one among the Huns who spoke comprehensible Italian, the colonel, told me that my child and I could sleep in the cheese hut. Until they might have need for it themselves.

"'Let me cook for you," I said. "Surely you'll need a cook."

"'We have our own cooks."

"'*Ma, io sono brava*," I told him. "I'm very good. Let me try. Give me a chance. What do your cooks know to do with our food? My baby girl and I would be no trouble if we stayed in the pantries off the kitchen. No trouble at all."

'Seeing he was convinced, I took another step. "And those two women," I said, pointing at Abriana and Tessa, who were trying to make themselves invisible, "it's they who keep the house clean, do the scrubbing, the laundry, the ironing."

"'We have our own systems, *signora*."

"'But the house is big, the work never-ending. We are used to it. They can sleep near my child and me. No trouble at all."

'Pursing his girlish lips, the colonel nodded once again. I tried for one last concession. "There are two old men in the olive mill. One is my father, one is my husband's father. They began yesterday to press this year's harvest.

Our oil is the best in the region. Oh, it is. And they will milk the cows, groom your horses. We need them. I know that you have men who can do this work. But not as well as they can."

"'No trouble at all? In the pantries off the kitchen?" he asked.

"'Yes." I knew it would be warm there in that space, that I would have first access to supplies, theirs and ours. To feed my own. My family had been decreased to five.

'What I recall most about those first days of living with the Huns was the lavish hysteria with which they ate and drank, their need for food and drink orgiastic. Supply trucks came regularly up the white road, unloading potatoes and cabbages, cabbages, endless crates of them, sacks of flour, barrels of wine, casks of grappa, animals on the hoof and those just slaughtered, still bleeding as they heaved them onto the pantry floors, often splattering the small bed I'd set up there for Filippa. Sometimes there were crates of seafish and clams and mussels, fresh and pulsing under their cover of salt-smelling weeds, though how such miraculous goods were acquired I could never imagine. What with my subtle pilfering, we ate more and better than we had before they came. But the days of plenty were only a precursor to a longer epoch of agony.

'The treasures we'd so carefully buried were early on discovered, devoured. The more they found, the more they wanted. Once while Tessa was soaping laundry in the wash house, one of the nine stomped in, took her by the scruff of the neck. Lifting her off the ground, throwing her down near one of the ditches where some stores had been buried, he pushed her to her knees, bent her face to the dirt, held her there, telling her to sniff out the rest. How they laughed, slapping one another, snorting, outdoing one another's small torments upon Tessa. Marco-Tullio had been witness for most of this scene. Understanding that his attempt to rescue Tessa would result in amusement more tragic, he remained apart. It was the final spur, I think, to his collaboration with the Partigiani.

'He'd collect eggs in the morning, put a few aside, hide some of the fruit he collected from the cellars before each meal, wrap half a loaf from every day's bake and stash it away. On the evenings when he deemed his sack full enough, he would help me to put Filippa to sleep, gather his things and be off, never knowing if the camps had been abandoned, the Partigiani's position changed, who he would find or where. He would smile when I'd beg him not to go, tell me that those men up there in the mountains were trying to rid his country of the Hun and that maybe an egg or two might help. On the morning he was brought back to the villa by a Partigiano, the colonel offered me two lackeys to dig my father's grave. Refusing him as kindly as I could, Battista and Abri and I took turns with the spade against the near-frozen January earth. I washed my father in oil, sewed him a shroud from sheets, and we laid him in one of the ditches he'd helped to dig months before in which to hide our food. It was in March that we buried him in a proper grave.

'I never believed my father's forays were limited to delivering eggs, and Ugo would later verify my suspicion.

'What would have been enough to keep the original thirty-eight of us through that winter until the earth would yield again, the nine finished off in six weeks. Maybe it was less than that. Even so—as I'd done from the first day—when I set to work each morning with the food that had been delivered for my "guests", I would keep two pots nearby into which I ladled and spooned portions of the Huns' supper for Filippa, Abri, Tessa and Battista. Surely the colonel knew that's how we kept alive but he never said, never forbade, never even let me know that he knew.

'It was the end of January when the supply trucks began to arrive less often. We slaughtered the last of the animals, even the milk cows, and wrung the necks of old hens. We lived on potatoes and apples and a thin soup of cornmeal. What saved us was our oil.

'I would place on the table an *anfora* of oil—a thing exotic to the Hun—show the men how to drizzle it over the potatoes, the soup, to enrich the poor food. Somehow I think the colonel took this gesture of mine about the oil as a kind of personal courtesy from me to him. Every evening, his lips pursed in the usual way, he would take up the *anfora* himself, walk around the table, delicately pouring it out for his men. This pleased him. As much, I think, as if he'd had a great haunch of venison to carve.

'One evening a soldier from the camps came rushing in, begging pardon, stumbling, saluting, announcing some sort of trouble among the men, but the colonel kept on with his ritual with the oil. Tessa and I were standing by while they dined, as we did each evening—serving, clearing, waiting—and when the colonel finished, he nodded at us, smiled his wet, womanish smile. Telling his men to proceed with their supper, only then did he look at the soldier, walk with him away from the table, listen to him, give his orders. All we heard the colonel say was, *Shoot them, Herkert. Every one of them if you must.*

'Before the soldier left, he turned, looked back at the men around the table, at their spooning up of what must have seemed a feast to him since by then they were eating roots and dirt in those camps. And with the same envious gaze which the dying have for those who will stay a while longer, the soldier looked at me. Feeling his eyes on me, I raised mine to him. In apology, I think. I felt sorry that he may have thought me shameless, pandering to the enemy. Courting them in a way. I felt sorry knowing that he was hungry. It was me who looked away first.

'Their evening meal finished, the nine would retire to the *salone* or to their rooms or, more often, to the brothel they'd arranged right here in the lodge. You'll forgive my nonchalance but, yes, right here in Biagino's little house the

Hun officers entertained village women and girls. Shocked, are you? That Italian women and girls were willing? To barter themselves for a sack of apples? *Dio buono*, a piece of cheese? Will you say they were *corrupt*? Would you call them whores? The penchant for corruption is human. War simply enlarges its reach. As I've said, you've never been hungry . . .

'Where was I then? As soon as the officers were gone, Abri and I would set the table for our own supper. I would serve it nicely, one thing at a time, the wan little soup and then the potatoes smashed with oil and salt, the skins fried in a little more oil or some other fat if we had it. Then the apples, cut thinly, sprinkled with sugar from the sack of it I'd stolen early on and stowed behind my bed. We would talk a bit, try for a bit of *brio*. For Filippa's sake if not for our own.

'I would eat a morsel, a spoonful, put aside the rest. I always saved something. For days on end I would feel nothing of hunger and then the ache of it would begin to gnaw. For a long time I could feed myself with dreams: *Ugo would arrive, the old truck sagging under the weight of sacks of flour and beans, cabbages and potatoes rolling about on the metal bed.* How quickly our fantasies turn humble. And when I could no longer remember the dream or no longer be swindled by it, I would creep down the steep, broken cellar steps, inhale the wine-dark smell of bruised fruit decaying on the stone floor. All the still-good apples already having been gathered up and taken to the table, what was left was half-fermented pulp, nibbled at by flies and rats, and I scooped it up, ate it from my palm. How angry I was with Ugo then. I grew to hate him, to blame him for leaving us to save others. Did he know the Huns were living in his home, did he know that his child and his father and his wife were starving? Was he twenty kilometres away? A thousand? Why didn't he send word, why didn't he come himself? I went so far as to wish him dead and then I would weep, praying that he wasn't.

'One evening at table, Filippa asked for cabbage. So much had it become part of our daily food, she missed it. Though I understood her yearnings were for more than cabbage, I think Filippa asked for it because it was the least of her desires. The only one that might be fulfilled.

'Tessa fixed her small Tartar eyes on mine. "I know where there are cabbages."

"'Where?'"

"'Still in the ground, in the patch near Tizianello.'"

"'It's an hour's walk there and back, and besides, I'm sure they're long gone, Tessa. No one would have been fool enough to leave them. And if someone did, someone else has found them by now. And even if you had the strength for such a journey and the cabbages were still there, have you forgotten that soldiers are camped all along that road? Soldiers who shoot anything that moves.'"

"'They'll all be asleep or drunk by the time I get there. I know what I'm doing.'"

"'But you don't, Tessa, you don't and I won't permit you to . . .'"

'Abri reached across the table, pressing the tips of her fingers on my hand. Eyes half-closed, nodding her head. "Let her go."

'Tessa went to Filippa then, took her in her arms, danced her about, tickling her, singing a song she called "Il valzer del cavolo", the Cabbage Waltz. It had been so long since I'd seen my baby girl giggle like that, throw her head back and laugh until the tears came.

'With Abri's sweater buttoned over her own, a shawl wrapped twice around her chest, her feet bound in rags inside rubber boots, a cloth sack and a knife in the pocket of her skirt, Tessa set out to find a cabbage for Filippa. It must have been ten, it might have been later as I stood on the veranda watching the small, wilful figure of her vanish down the white road.

'*There wasn't even a fox about, it was so still and I ran like the wind over the hard-packed paths through the trees, only taking the road for the last two kilometres. It was dark, low clouds hiding the moon. But when I reached the curve just before Tizianello, I saw there was a light burning in one of the windows upstairs, smoke puffing out the chimney. I went straight for the* orto *and there they were, a whole row of them looking like giant frozen roses. In case anyone might be looking out the window, I lay down on my belly, crawled along the cabbages. First I took the leaves which had fallen off, stuffed them in my sack, then I cut two heads. So big, there wasn't room for a third. Dragging the sack behind me, I pushed my way back to the edge of the* orto. *When I stood up, there he was. He'd been watching me, standing there smoking and watching me, and first I thought to run but the sack was too heavy and I wasn't leaving it, and then I thought to speak but nothing came out, and when he reached for me I thought it was all over but then I realised he was wiping the cold water and the mud from my hand—one hand, then the other—with the front of his sweater. This sweater.*

'Touching the front of a thick, dark grey Wehrmacht sweater so large and long on her small form it hung below her knees, she said, *He took it off himself and pulled it down over my head, all the while murmuring something, shaking his head. He motioned for me to stay still, raised his hand, then his finger.* Un augenblick, un momento, *he said, running to the house. Seconds later he came out with . . . with these. Look,* signora. *You won't believe it, I can hardly believe it. Look.* Guardate, guardate, she kept saying, hot triumphant tears streaming from the high slant of her Tartar eyes.

'From the sack, Tessa pulled a round of black bread, hard and shiny as polished stone but bread nevertheless. *Real bread.* Then came two tall thin jars of pink-cheeked apricots sealed with paraffin. A block of white butter wrapped in a rag. Had the soldier been home on leave? Was he a fresh recruit, newly posted in the Tuscan hills, sent off by his mother, his wife with these homey expressions of love? How strange, I'd thought, touching the wax plugs on the jars, food from Germany to feed a Tuscan family.

'I remember pleading with Tessa to be quiet, telling her that she'd wake Filippa and who knows which others and to take off her boots and let me warm her feet in my hands and would she drink a cup of sage tea before she slept? Tessa was beyond hearing me, though. Like a chalice, she held the butter high over her head, a prize she'd borne safely through the night, an enemy's gift bestowed with tender mercy and surely some measure of awe, I have always thought.

'The nine Huns who lived in the villa came and went, often remaining in Firenze for days, a week. Sometimes the supply truck would stop to make a delivery when they were gone and I was prudent with my thieving, cunning about my hiding. Once when they returned from Firenze or wherever they'd been the colonel wasn't with them. Another officer, one I'd never seen before, seemed to be in charge. He spoke no Italian and our few, brief encounters were conducted in gestures. All the *danke schön*s and *bitte*s gone away with him, I understood that the colonel had performed as a kind of house mother to his men as much as a commanding officer. The men he left behind fell into decline. Was it adolescent rebellion now that the martinet colonel was no longer? Perhaps. More, it was their turn to suffer thinning illusions. The Huns were losing.

'As soon as the threat of frost was gone and a hoe could break the earth, we planted. One morning when I was sowing rows of peas and lettuces, I heard a strange but familiar *Buongiorno, signora*. I looked up to see our *fattore* standing there. Biagio's father. He was called Felice. Happiness. He and his wife—she was Annarosa—and Biagio had been among those who'd come to live with us in the villa until the Huns arrived and turned them out that first day of December. When they'd returned to their farmhouse, Felice began to tell me, they'd found it ransacked, burned, *invivible*. Unliveable. The three fled somewhere to the east—Le Marche, I think—to family there. Yet there he was on that late March morning, dear Felice, already bending down to take over my handiwork, pushing the seeds into the dirt his way, speaking in a soft, strained voice.

'"I wanted Annarosa to stay a while longer with her family but she's come back with me. When I smelled the spring close by I couldn't stay away. And Biagio, almost fifteen now, *signora*. Wait until you see him. We'll get to planting two, maybe three wheatfields, however many we can manage, the two of us. And we'll get to the vines and the olives need pruning and Annarosa will help you to put in the garden and I couldn't stay away any longer, I'd prefer to die here than away from here and I don't give a good damn about the Huns and I heard about your father, *signora*, we heard and . . ."

'As he wept through his broken words, I started in weeping with him, we two squatting in the damp black just-turned earth. It was spring and Felice was there with me and we'd sow and maybe live long enough to reap and life might become something like it had been before.

'"I brought you this. From my wife's sister, *signora*. Made before the war." From the sack on his back Felice took a small, cloth-wrapped cheese, held it out to me.

'Tessa, Abri, Battista, Filippa and I sat on the hard-packed earth outside the wine shed that day, Battista gouging pieces of the cheese and offering it to us on the point of his knife. Silent ghosts, we sat there leaning against the old wooden hut, closing our eyes to the glory of the stuff, pressing at the crumbs fallen on our palms, sucking them from our fingers; I can still taste that cheese made of wild grasses, earth, rock, sun, the dust of just-cut wheat, rain-wet flocks, oakwood smoke, all of it was there rolling around in my mouth. It still does, sometimes it does.

'Did I tell you that Biagio's mother was called Annarosa? A beautiful name. Once a day, sometimes more, Abri and I would go to her, try to make some little progress in restoring their *casolare*. It's the house where Biagio and Giorgia live now, you know. Mostly in vain we worked with Annarosa, the cool green air flapping the fire-scorched curtains against the shards of windowpanes while we swept and scrubbed. Having begged Annarosa and Felice to share the rooms off the kitchen with us, telling them the Huns wouldn't care or likely notice, still they refused. As long as they had water, Felice said, they could manage. Washing pots and clothes and themselves in an old marble sink open to the sky in what was once the kitchen, they set up beds in a room that still had a roof and Annarosa cooked in a firepit she'd dug in the yard. That was in

April. Certain events in June would cause Felice to change his mind about coming to live in the villa.

'What with the *orto* beginning to yield and the regular arrival of the Huns' supplies, hunger was replaced by another nightmare, the growing savagery of our guests. The Huns stopped bathing and leaving their laundry in piles on their bedroom floors to be washed. After their manoeuvres or whatever it was that kept them away during most of the day, they would rumble back to the villa, tear open their tunics, break the necks of bottles with their knives—less trouble than a corkscrew. But their real sport was shooting. Floors, walls, paintings, mirrors. Shadows. More than once, each other. As though if they didn't hone their inhumanity they might turn into men, the Huns shot off their pistols. Sometimes I wondered if they would grow weary of being fiends or of playing the role of fiends but they never did.

'When they'd design to leave the brothel or their rooms to come to table, the reek of the Huns was vile, the taint of dirty wool over unwashed flesh. Their boots were shiny enough, though. They'd sit for hours with rags and little tins of polish, another tin of something to clean the metal of their buckles. Medals in a row, faces shaved, hair stinking of sweat, slicked neat with water. Goatish brutes who were losing their war, nothing could hide how foul they were.

'It was June. The Allies had invaded Europe via Normandy, the Americans were on their way up the peninsula from Sicilia, and—having pitilessly vanquished the Huns—the Russians were moving east. *Quasi finito*, almost over; we said it to one another with our eyes, a furtive laugh. *Quasi finito*.

'Meanwhile the *orto* was thriving, Tessa, Abri and I harvesting peas and lettuces, early beans, onions, zucchini twice a day, and what with those and the berries and grasses we foraged and the foods which were ported up the white road by who knows what villainy, I think we became somehow dazzled by the plenty, by the real cooking and baking we could once again plunge into. If never in our hearts, in our ways and means we'd *adapted* to life with the Huns.

'Under the new command, one of our daily tasks was to scrub the lodge, bring down some food, see to it that the wine barrel was replenished. I loathed setting foot in the Hun trysting place but the work itself was simple enough and wanted less than an hour. Once the villa was somewhat in order, I would almost look forward to the walk down to the lodge and back again. Sometimes Abri or Tessa would accompany me, but mostly I would go alone, leaving Filippa in the care of one of them or Battista.

'It was nearing the end of June that day, already sultry by eleven in the morning. I remember thanking the gods for the sun's heat on my face as I walked down the hill. Setting down my baskets, taking off my sweater and tying it around the waist of my dress, I felt fine. In a way, fine. I wasn't halfway to the lodge when I heard Tessa shouting from behind me, "*Aspetta, aspettami.*"

'I sat for a moment on the stones until she caught up with me and we went together to the lodge, set to working, Tessa scrubbing the floors while I began changing linens, grumbling that the Huns—themselves unwashed—would lie with their paramours—they, too, most likely unwashed—upon sheets we scrubbed until our hands bled and laid to dry over wild rosemary bushes. Lost in the irony of that, it was Tessa who heard them first.

'Jeeps or trucks, a motorcycle, I thought. On the creek road. Strange at this hour unless they were bringing supplies or people up to the villa. We went to the door to see. The oaks in summer leaf hid whatever, whoever it was, but voices, shouting, drunken, reached us clearly.

'"Tessa, run. Go. Out the back door and into the woods, towards the hunters' trail. Wait for me there. You know what to do, you know how to make yourself invisible. You know what to do, Tessa. I'll find you. Go, Tessa. Now."

'Shaking her head, defiance glittering daggers in her eyes, "I'm not leaving you."

'"Alone I can manage them. *Corri*. Run." I watched her start up the pinewood path then turned to see that there were six of them. Bottles of whisky in one hand, pistols in the other, they were shouting for the night girls who they somehow thought would be there at eleven in the morning.

'"*Liebchen. Schöne mädchen.*"

'As they entered, I made no move save to untie my sweater from my waist, slip my arms through the sleeves. I began to button it. I did this slowly, my eyes roving over each of them, daring them. Giving Tessa time. At first struck dumb by what they must have thought was my fearlessness, one of them came closer and then the others did, surrounding me, greeting me salaciously, offering me their bottles, running open hands down my thighs, across my breasts. One stayed near the door. From there, he shouted something above the din of the others, shouted again. Shooting his pistol in the air to quiet them, he said the words once more. That last time almost in a whisper. I think he told them they should leave me be, that I was already spoken for by one of the officers. It was something like that, for the others broke the circle around me, turned back to their bottles, threw themselves on the beds, put their pistols down long enough to light cigarettes. As I buttoned the last button on my sweater I looked at the man who'd calmed them; nodding to him, I walked out the door.

'Once I was certain to be out of sight, I ran. Across the meadow to a rocky trail through the hills and up towards the feet of the mountains where the farmers hunt deer. Calculating the distance Tessa would have covered by then, I thought to intercept her. I would reach the first fork in the pinewood path even before she had. "*Corri, corri da* Tessa. Run, run to Tessa," I kept saying to myself through my breathlessness. But my mind was screaming with other commands, flashing blurred scenes like a film on the wrong speed. Still I ran, until some force—some *compulsion*—led me off the trail, into the pathless woods where the boar live. Only patches of ground were trampled enough for me to pass through the density of the underbrush. Making my way back to the trail, this time I didn't run away from the lodge but traversed the meadow which leads to it.

'Did I know? Was it Tessa clawing, blaspheming, spitting at the Huns? Were those the images that made me fly over the meadows? Above the vicious thudding of my heart, I could hear them laughing as I neared the lodge. Barbarous, rutting laughs.

'I saw them standing near the door. And then I saw her. Save shreds of her blouse, Tessa was naked, impaled below her breasts on the point of a bayonet, hanging on the lodge door. The day's trophy. Smaller than a fawn. In a kind of queue, the men were waiting their turn. I knelt in the dirt and rocked myself, biting my fingers, eyes closed against what they'd seen. If I kept my eyes closed, I could make the scene vanish. Even until now, it has never vanished. Why did she go back to the lodge? I know why. She came to see that I was safe. Tessa came back for me.

'The soldier who had earlier warned them away from me was screaming at the men to stop, pulling one and then another away from the dead Tessa. He ran then, towards the creek road, but I knew that he'd be back. I knew it and, still crouching, I waited for him. It seemed such a long time that I waited but then I saw him. No pistol this time, he pointed another kind of gun. He strafed the men, strewed them over the stones. Down her thighs, I saw Tessa's blood dripping through their slime.

'The soldier removed the bayonet, took Tessa's body in his arms. Together we wrapped her in one of the rosemary-perfumed sheets meant for the Hun beds. I sat with Tessa while the soldier went for his jeep. Driving it over the stones, through the bushes, he stopped close to the lodge door. We placed Tessa in the back of the jeep and I knelt next to her, my arms around her. I hummed the tune she'd made up for Filippa. I sang the Cabbage Waltz.

'The soldier and I took Tessa into the wine shed. Abri was nowhere to be seen but Battista and Filippa were walking towards us from the villa until I shouted at him to take my baby girl back into the house. He hesitated then turned around, lifting Filippa onto his shoulders. The soldier stood guard by the wine-shed door until I returned with oil, clean clothes and rags. I had no candles and the only soap we had was what we'd made from wood ash and olive oil. I washed her, rubbed oil into the scant flesh of her, dressed her, rebraided her hair. We wrapped her in a quilt, carried her into the villa through the kitchen door, laid her on her bed. I stayed with her to wait for Abri. At some point during the vigil the soldier went away and I never saw him again. Who was he? Why did he do what he did? Wouldst the gods gift me another day to live for every time I've wondered about him. I think what happened was that he'd reached the confines of his own endurance for what he'd seen. Maybe for what he'd done. He crossed over into another place where he was no longer a soldier of the Wehrmacht but simply a man. A good man. Has the memory of him softened my German odium? From time to time, it has. Until I hear Tessa singing to Filippa, dancing about the kitchen with her that night. Until then.

'Nor did any one of us ever see Abri again. Not after that afternoon when she returned from helping Annarosa.

I didn't tell Abri what happened to Tessa but made up a story about her being caught in crossfire. No words, no screams, she bent to kiss her daughter. And then she was gone. After the war, people said that she had gone up into the hills to fight, that she stayed there, died there. I believe that, but I don't know it. I have never regretted lying to Abri. Never once. Not so about other of my lies.

'I didn't tell Battista the truth about Tessa either, nor anyone else until years later when I told Ugo. And long after that, I told Biagio. I don't want people to know and yet I don't want what happened not to be remembered. I don't want that at all.

'It was Battista and I who buried Tessa next to Marco-Tullio; more Battista than I. A man unused to wielding a shovel, he prepared the grave, gathered flowers, lamented the lack of a coffin. He wept. Not even when Tancredi or Maria-Luce died had I seen him in that collapsing kind of agony with which he grieved for Tessa. As I watched him, words from the past, glances, things said, not said tumbled into another pattern. Was it Battista who had fathered Tessa? Were he and Abri lovers and was that the reason Abri mourned so desperately when Maria-Luce died? Was it that Abri regretted her betrayal of the woman who was a mother to her, the woman who never even asked her to reveal the name of the man who fathered her child? Did Maria-Luce already know? How many lies and secrets are taken to the grave?

'I never learned who disposed of the slaughtered men at the lodge or whether the officers who lived at the villa ever knew about the "incident". None of them spoke of that morning to me or, as far as I know, to anyone else. What I *did* know was that if the Partigiani were suspected of the killings, there would be reprisals. Ten Italians for every German. That was the rule. Instead, as though nothing ever happened on that June morning at the lodge, there were no words, no threats, no revenge. The Huns, us—as I've said, I think we were all ghosts by then. I would walk down to the lodge each morning, fix a few wildflowers to that place on the door and they were always there, untouched, when I returned the next day. I don't know if the lodge was used by the Huns after that. I don't think it was. No one ever asked me to resume my work there, perhaps knowing I would refuse if they did.

'It was then that Felice, Annarosa and Biagino came to live in the villa with us. After Tessa died. It's interesting to think of our ages at that time. Tessa had been sixteen.

Abri was thirty-three, Filippa five, Biagio fifteen and I was twenty-four. The elders of the small tribe were Annarosa and Felice, at forty-five, and Battista at sixty-three.'

As Antonia has been speaking, her face, her gestures, the lines of her body have been transformed. First to a greater age and then back to her present one; most curious of all, much of the time she has seemed eerily like a girl. Like the twenty-four-year-old Antonia rebraiding Tessa's hair.

'It was on the day when they were leaving Castelletto. In the early morning before the light came on the day when the Huns went away. It was the eleventh of August 1944, a week after Firenze had been liberated by the Allies, that acting as the undisputed goad to their quitting Castelletto and Toscana and likely Italy itself. But I didn't know that then as I lay still, listening to the ruckus of their departure.

'The shouting, the starting up of motors, boots crunching on the stones and pounding up the stairs and down; I could smell them. I could always smell them.

There are times still when I walk through to the *dispensa* or when I'm up in the *mansarda* and I think to catch a whiff, some hideous breath of them swirling, corrupting.

'As it happened, Filippa had been feverish the night before and she and I had gone to bed soon after I'd served and cleared for the Huns. Sleeping on her side, her two plump arms twined around one of mine, her face was hot against my shoulder. I picked her up, carried her—still sleeping, her long legs dangling at my waist—to the basin of water on the windowsill. I bathed her head, her face, her proud little chest, and returned to bed with her.

'It was the second day, maybe the third, of the wheat harvest and I listened as Felice and Annarosa and Biagio prepared to leave for the fields, and to Battista, who would accompany them that day as an extra hand. Knowing Filippa was not well, they moved about quietly, and quieter still had they left the villa.

'I always pushed a dresser in front of the door before Filippa and I would settle abed. Now, in a single thrust, the dresser toppled and he stood there. No, he *posed*. Closed the door. It was Herkert. The one who'd come to speak to the colonel, the one who'd looked at me with a dying man's eyes that evening in the *salone* months before.

'*Occhi azzurri*. Eyes the colour of a May sky. A headful of blond curls. He gagged me with some vile cloth, tied my wrists to the bedposts, took Filippa—already stunned into that silent kind of terror—from the bed and tied her to her little chair, securing the ropes to the handle of the door so she sat at a forward incline, straining like a puppy tethered too short. He took his filthy handkerchief from his pocket, tied it around her mouth and I could see her struggling to breathe. Then he took what he'd come to take from me. Hauling himself up, he threw me from the bed to the floor, then strung me up in a rocking position—ensuring my immobility—and tied me to the claw foot of the bed. He walked to the door, patted Filippa on the head, she still silent save her gasping breath. Laughing, he dumped the basin of water over her, laughing harder as she gulped and choked, watching her until her head fell limp, her struggling ceased. Straightening his clothes, he stood there looking at her. How sated he seemed, what with his seed spent and having murdered such a tiny girl without so much as dirtying his hands. He turned to me, pulled a pistol from its holster, aimed, his hand moving in time to his blood-soaked laugh. He shot. "*Auf weidersehen, meine liebe.*"

'All I can remember of that first instant after he'd gone was shouting to Filippa, from behind the rag in my mouth, "*Guardami. Guardami, amore mio, guarda la mamma.*"

'A lifetime passed before she lifted her head and opened her eyes, only the whites showing. I never stopped my garbled begging. *Look at me, my love. Look at your mamma.*

'Even now when I watch Filippa, especially when she is across a room or just coming through a door, I see my five-year-old baby girl, see her eyes rolling like that. Hear that silent cry. And sometimes when I look at Luce, I . . . Have you ever noticed the blue of Luce's eyes? Blue as a May sky.

'I will never know if Filippa lost consciousness from time to time or remained aware through all those hours afterwards. Nine hours. I would faint and come to and see her sitting there rocking her tiny self as much as the ropes would allow. I think she keened or that I did. Maybe it was how we comforted each other. I can recall very little. I knew that Filippa was still alive and I believed that my noise, my incomprehensible pleading, would keep her so.

'I was aware enough at some point to feel the pain in my leg, the blood trickling from it, and aware enough, too, to begin trying to sort out what had happened. Not so much what, but *why*. Was his visit a quickly executed revenge upon the woman who had excluded him from the comforts of her table on that evening when he'd come to speak with the colonel? Excluded him, perhaps, from her bed? Is that what he'd thought? Or was his design far more grotesque? Was it Filippa he wanted? I think it was. The luscious pleasure of murdering a child, and for an added pungency, to do it while her mother looked on. I am certain—have always been certain—that Herkert meant to kill Filippa and believed he had. And that he did not mean to kill me but to leave me in the living death of watching my baby die.

'Do you remember that first evening when you came to dine, when Filippa and Luce sat with us around the fire? Do you remember what I said about the bastard Hun's impulse to ruthlessness? Their obscenities have an intellectual rub. A scholarly bestiality, theirs. Years later I would read of Mengele's calling for a cellist to play Schumann in his laboratory while he sat dissecting the little corpses of twins he'd just murdered. An oversight, perhaps, that he'd not invited their mother in to observe.

'But how did Herkert know where to find me? As though my name was on the door and he knew the way through the labyrinth of the villa straight to it, how did he know? Did he conspire with one of the officers, who led him to me? Perhaps whole days have passed in the sixty years since then during which I have not relived that morning, but not so many of them.

'It was Biagio who found us. Always announcing himself long before he reached the villa, I'd heard him shouting for me from the oak walk, "*Signora, signora. Ho trovato funghi precoci.* I've found early mushrooms."

'Over and over again I heaved my body against the bed, but of course that made not enough noise to tell him where I was. I waited then, willing him to pass through the kitchen, the pantries, and finally he did. He knocked. He banged, screamed. Threw open the door. When he saw that Filippa was tied to it, he knelt to her. Biagio knew that the best way to help me was to save Filippa and the first thing he did was to kiss her, to speak softly to her while he loosed the ropes, untied the cloth from her mouth, took her in his arms, Filippa drooping like a rag doll split open at the neck.

'"*Tutto va bene, signora, tutto va bene*," he told me as he laid her down on the bed, rubbed her wrists, put her on his shoulder and bounced her, kissing her, crooning to her, anything to get her to make a sound. Finally she began to cry. Filippa still in his arms, Biagio came to me then, began trying to work the knots when Annarosa came in.

'Taking Filippa from her son, she gave triage orders: *Heat water, pour it in that jug, bring soap from the washhouse; bring oil, bring sheets from the armoire; go to find your father; where is* signor *Battista?*

'Annarosa sat Filippa on the bed, put her ear to her chest, listened, counted beats, told her to breathe deeply, more deeply, all the while saying, *Brava, bravissima*. I remember she asked Filippa to tell her a story so she could hear her speak, listen to her pronunciation of the words. While Filippa told the story, Annarosa washed her, caressed her slowly with the oil, dressed her in the clothes that were still folded on the windowsill where I'd left them the evening before. By then Felice and Battista had arrived and untied me, carried me to the bed so that I could touch Filippa, talk to her while Annarosa dressed her. The mass of her ringlets so black against the pallor of her face, her eyes made of a thousand blues when she turned to look at me, Filippa laid her hand on my arm.

'It was Felice who declared my wound a graze. Washing my leg, disinfecting it with grappa, he held me up to sip from a small glass of the same, sat me in a chair with my leg out straight while he and Biagio changed my sheets. I can recall each detail of those ministrations they performed for Filippa and for me that afternoon. Mostly I can hear their voices.

'No one asked questions. Not even Annarosa did as she washed me later, pulled a fresh white nightdress over my head. Fed me sage tea with an egg. They didn't need to know what happened as much as they needed to help. After all, they were Tuscan.

'The malaise about us lingered. Moving among the others, I spoke in nods and weak smiles. She screaming if anyone but Biagio or I touched her, I held Filippa in my arms no matter what else I had the strength to do. Even she and I spoke only in that mute language of the desolate, saying all we had to say by staying close. A week passed, two; still Filippa shunned the company of everyone save Biagino, clinging to him as she did to me, hiding her face in his shoulder. He would carry her down to the creek or into the orchards, sit her on the grass, weave wildflowers in her hair. She smiled only for him, sang soft songs to her soup rather than sipping it. She slept.

'After having been gone nearly eleven months, Ugo came home on the twelfth of September. To put it another way, it was a month after Herkert's visit to my room when Ugo returned. I already knew I was carrying Herkert's child. I knew it in my heart. We always do, I think we do. Had Ugo not come home so soon after Herkert, would life have taken a different path?

'In the days between Herkert and Ugo, I'd worked my way through six or eight or more scenarios: what I would tell him, what I would keep from him; would he return to find my belly swollen? a babe in my arms? But when I saw him, when I caught first sight of him, I knew what I would do.

Wild hair more grey than brown, bearded, skinny and long as an old bony fish, he was beautiful. Beautiful Ugo was, and even as I ran towards him down the oak road, my untied hair flying in the hot September wind, bare feet scudding over the white stones, I knew what I would do. And so I did.

'Ugo bent over the pallet in the kitchen where Filippa was inclined to spend her days. She opened her eyes. She looked at him, scurried out from the covers, held her arms up to him. Safe upon the refuge of his chest, she covered his face with kisses. Over every centimetre of it she made little puffs with her dry cherry lips, stopping now and then to look hard into his eyes before she resumed the earnest demonstration of her love. Placing her little brown hands on his cheeks, she commanded, "*Mai più, papà. Non puoi lasciarmi mai più.* Never again, *papà*. You can't leave me ever again."

'"*Mai*, Filippetta. Never."

'"You must sleep with Mamma and me."

'"I will."

'"I must be in the middle."

'"You shall."

'I told Ugo about Herkert. I wanted him to defend me. Not to track down Herkert and murder him, nothing like that. I wanted more: I wanted Ugo to defend my *goodness*, goodness being larger than innocence. I wanted Ugo to be my cavalier, jumping the moat, waving my colours. Yes, I think that's it. Don't we all want that? As much, we want pity. And what did Ugo want? Aloud he never said. Without words, what he clamoured for was *my* pity. Pity is a woman's gift, you know. More than round breasts and strong hips and fine Titian flanks, it's pity a man desires. And it's pity a man cannot give. As though I'd killed Tancredi, seduced Herkert, called down the war and all its savagery, Ugo would have me comfort *him*. Yes, silently he entreated my pity. Had I withheld it or asked *his* pity for me, he would have looked away from me. Sooner or later, he would have done that. Perhaps he did anyway. Ewes stay. Rams wander.

'As it neared the time for my baby to be born, Ugo's desire was that we tell it a pretty story, say that its real *papà* was a handsome blond soldier who died in the war. I couldn't face that. *You are her father. Make that the truth.*

'Luce was born on April twenty-eighth. Anyone who might have been calculating the time from when Ugo returned until her birth would have been comfortable enough believing he had fathered her. To the rumourists who whispered my baby had been conceived on the morning when the Huns went away, the measuring of time would have left them equally comfortable believing *that* was true. What was indisputable was that little Luce was in my image just as was Filippa.

'*You are her father. Make that the truth*, I begged Ugo time and again, tempting him to it with that pity for which he yearned. My pity was the price of Ugo's lie.

'Our post-war life was devoted to the restoration of the farms and the raising up of the old stone houses from ruins. The number of Castelletto men who died in battle, in German prisoner-of-war camps or in the Resistenza was high: eleven men lost. In the scheme of the fifty-five million who died, a modest number? Not when one understands that we were a family who lost eleven sons. Eleven sons and Marco-Tullio. Over time, the men, women and children who survived came marching home and, each time one did, there was a great rejoicing. Another lamb back safe in the fold.

'The fields, the vines and orchards were nearly in order by the spring of 1946 and new barns had been constructed for the animals that Battista and Ugo began to acquire, while the work on the farmhouses would want nearly a decade to complete, leaving certain of the families to live in the villa with us until 1955. Perhaps for longer than that.

'Throughout those years Felice was the hero. The land, the rebuilding, the comfort of the farmers, all thrived under his reign, and always Biagio was by his side. Together with Battista and Ugo, it was Felice who began, slowly at first, to retract the sharecropping agreements with the farmers, take them on as day workers to be paid monthly stipends, thus making Castelletto one of the first large holdings on the peninsula to abolish the *mezzadria*.

'For Ugo and me it was a time of joy restrained. Suffering on the wane, still we were wary, sleeping with our boots on, our guns under the pillow. If only metaphorically, I still do. I still wake in the night thinking to hear one of those blood-soaked voices: *Bun jhorn'-o, seegnorrah.*

'Luce was balm to Filippa's inevitable wounds, a tiny beautiful creature to love and cherish. I wondered then and do now if Filippa, in her own bravely managed tristesse, sensed that little Luce had also been marked somehow. Dishonoured. Did Filippa whisper her secrets to the baby? I used to think she did and wished she would to me so I might comfort her. Rather Filippa soothed herself by soothing Luce.

'Me, I was taken up almost wholly with forgetting: Filippa tied to the chair; Herkert's eyes; Tessa. Angry with Ugo for being himself—taciturn, solitary—for resuming, once again, his travels, I had already extracted my pound of flesh for his lie, so how could I ask for more? What made me think I *deserved* it? Tancredi having set up house with us early on, now there was Herkert, moved in to stay.

'Luce must have been nearly two, Filippa eight, when one morning Ugo was again preparing for a journey. Though by then he'd told me of his work with the OSS, his involvement before and during the war, had explained there were certain ongoing projects in which he would continue to participate, his travels always held for me some aura of a lark, of escape, a scorning of me. That particular morning, his hair still damp from the bath, a creamy white silk shirt in his hand, he turned to me, asked me to accompany him. Having never been further away than Firenze, I was stunned and timid; thrilled, yes, but thunderstruck.

'"The children?"

'"Annarosa will stay with them."

'"Where? Where are you going?"

'"To Paris. I have some business but not so much that we wouldn't be together, especially in the evenings."

'Tattered, moody, the war still fresh on her face, Paris wore weariness and rapture with the same swagger and I admired her more than I liked her. We followed Ugo's private map of the place. As we walked backstreets, past rubble-filled husks of buildings, he would point to upper-floor rooms on the blackened facades of others where he'd hidden, slept, waited. His haunts were still there, some of them, cafés with long zinc bars behind which rouged and flame-haired patronesses of a certain age pulled down the white porcelain handles of beer kegs, ran their splayed palms listlessly over their breasts.

'I'd wind and twist my hair into elaborate chignons, draw a thin black line along my eyelids, run my little finger through a pot of rouge and over my lips. Chinese red, I think it was called. I'd wear the same black dress every evening, one of Maria-Luce's. Padded shoulders, a heart-shaped bodice, it was of black faille and I'd always thought it too short, too smooth against my hips for Firenze. I felt fine in it there, a good Paris costume for a twenty-seven-year-old farmer's daughter from the mountains of Tuscany. Even my shoes had once been Maria-Luce's. In the rue du Bac, Ugo bought me my first pair of silk stockings and the contraption necessary to hold them up, black lace gloves, a velvet hair band with a short black spotted veil in which my eyelashes would catch, causing me to remain wide-eyed while Ugo laughed aloud. I couldn't recall then if I'd heard him laugh since before the war. I don't think I had.

'It wasn't that Ugo and I fell in love in Paris that first time but rather that we came to understand that we were. We drank in the rue du Temple because we liked it there and, as much, because we liked the long walk back to St.-Germaine-des-Prés where we dined at Lipp. I ate the same supper every time: *celeri remoulade, confit de canard, mille-feuilles à la crème pâtissière.* For all the years that followed, for all the times Ugo and I returned to Paris and to Lipp, that was always my supper. I should like to have it again.

'Ugo would chide me for my loping six-foot-woman's strides as we walked along the avenues, urge me to adopt the mincing derrière-swing of the Parigine. I tried once or twice but couldn't manage it. As I think about it, even my walk was conditioned by Herkert. Surely my lovemaking was. Did I invite him into my room that morning? Innocent, unwitting? Are there deeds innocent or unwitting? My own or anyone's? I've come to doubt it and so I ask myself, was it some gesture of mine, did I look at him for too long that first evening, did I flaunt what I'd provided to the others and denied to him, was it me who called down that disgrace upon my baby and myself?

'In the thirty-one years that I was married to Ugo we found day-by-day life mostly to our pleasure. Travelling well together, we did so now and then, renting the same rooms in Taormina every February, taking the girls to ski in the Dolomiti or to walk the *sentieri* in the Engadina. I suppose I can't say precisely when Ugo had become domesticated, but he seemed ever more taken up with the girls, with me, with the farms.

'We rode together, swam in the sea, worked in the *orto* and the fields, read, talked, schemed, received our friends and went about among them. In our pacific way, we battled. Ugo had even taken to sitting on a towel-covered armchair by the great square tub in our bathroom, sipping whisky while I bathed in the evenings. One would have had to know Ugo in his youth to understand how out of character a scene like that would have been.

'We were dancing. Not such a rare event. We danced always at the *sagre*. You know, that sort of country dancing which is always some kind of polka, I guess, mechanical, stiff. Pulling me close, he began to sing, his mouth close to my ear. Softly. A melody out of tune, out of pace with the chuffing in and out of the accordion.

'"*Non ti scordar di me. La vita mia è legata a te. Io t'amo sempre più, nel sogno mio rimani tu. Non ti scordar di me.* Don't forget me. My life is attached to yours. I love you always more and, in my dreams, you're always there." His cheek on my cheek, he sang every word of every stanza and I couldn't tell if the tears were mine or his.

"'How can I forget you when you're always attached to my hip? You don't leave me time to forget you, darling boy," I told him, my mind already thrashing at the vague whisper death makes. The accordion was onto another tune and still he held me.

"'I'm here to tell you that I shall be less present. It seems I am urgently required. On the other side. Not a long wait before I leave."

'My mother, Tancredi, Maria-Luce, Marco-Tullio, Tessa—it's not as though I'd never met with death, never grieved. Yet when Ugo died I tore my hair, beat my fists, keened my way through nights and days. I think it was the speed of it all that left me reeling—diagnosis, acceptance, his will not to linger, not to wait. He would have the last word rather than give it up to the Fates. If he must be done with life, it would be on his terms. I was sitting up in bed, he lying in my arms, his head against my breast. We were talking but I can't tell you about what. I remember asking him if he was cold. His body felt so cold. I remember that.

Death found Ugo while we slept that night. Did we talk about Herkert, Ugo and I? Did he long to tell Filippa and Luce the truth? Had the lie become the truth by then or did he die with a stone on his heart? Will I?

'Viola, Isotta, Sabina, their pallets on the floor around my bed, they kept a vigil. What were they then, ten, eight? Sabina, barely six? *Nonna, shall we tell you a story? Nonna, tonight can we sleep up in your bed?* How shocked I was at my egotism when the realisation finally broke through that those three little girls had lost their grandfather. Luce and Filippa their father. The only father either of them had ever known.

'A year later, Battista died on the day before his ninety-third birthday. His heiress, I was left the wealthiest forager in Tuscany, with all this land and my two brown dresses, my mother-in-law's wardrobe and what few of her jewels I'd yet to gift my daughters. Yes, those and the long sable coat Ugo had brought home for me only days before he died.

'Ugo had prepared me, advised me, drawn minutely detailed lists of what I was to do, not do, who I was to trust. To this day, Ugo is my guide through the inevitable machinations of running a farm as large as Castelletto.

Not to speak of a family as complex as mine. Umberto and the girls think they're doing things their way and mostly I let that grand falsity pass, though there isn't a wheel of cheese that's sold or a window repaired, a field planted, without my sanction, silent or otherwise. Mine and Biagino's.'

As she moved from scene to scene of her story, Antonia paced the room. Pouring out undrunk tea from the blue and white pot into a jug, she places it in the refrigerator, refills the kettle, makes fresh tea only to leave this, too, undrunk. From the still-untouched *pagnotta* which Biagio had brought that morning, she rips small pieces and, as though fixing them for a child, sprinkles sugar over them. For her child? For the child *she* was? Never was?

She walks to the open door of the lodge, tilts her head to the sky, closes her eyes to the thrumming of the nightbirds, the wing beat of owls settling upon a high branch of a pine. Walking out onto the stones, she welcomes the arrival of the stars, announces Venere, Sagitta and later, when the moon rises, Capricornus.

She must walk down to the creek at some point, so long is she gone, but it never occurs to me to follow. The white dust of the dry road on her boots when she returns, she walks to the princess bed, lays herself on the bare mattress, curls on her side and weeps. Taking a pillow from the pile I made earlier of the bed linen, I lift her head, slide the pillow under it. Raising my hand as though to place it on her forehead, I interrupt the gesture, quickly moving my hand to my cheek as though that was what I meant to do. Looking at me, understanding, she takes my hand, pulls it down to rest on her head, holds it there, covering my hand with hers. Knowing I don't need to speak for her to hear me, I stay silent. When she releases my hand, she turns on her back, covers her forehead with a folded arm, shielding her eyes though only a single candle lights the room. After a time she rises, smooths her brown dress, her hair, adjusts the tortoiseshell pins.

'Pentimento. Do you know the word?'

'Remorse.'

'Penance. Also that. But to a painter, pentimento is an underlying image, a painting under a painting, a fragment of a painting that shows through when the last layer of paint has become transparent with age. Have I become transparent with age? Secrets, lies showing through, are they? And is it remorse that I feel? Is it penance that the gods are asking of me? I, of myself?

'There it is. The marrow. The longing I couldn't name. It's *to know*, *to know for sure*, what is the right thing. With my lies, have I forfeited *the right thing*? I used to think my mother treacherous for her secrets yet here I am, my treachery greater, I think, if treachery can be measured. Is mine a coward's rationale, withholding to protect? And who is it I think to protect? My girls? Myself? I don't know. Luce is fifty-eight years old and I'll be damned if I can say she would be more harmed than not by knowing her father was my rapist, that he attempted to murder her sister, that he was likely mad with fear and drink and maybe his own kind of grief. Darling Lucetta. How hard it's been to love her. I've never understood if that's been true because she's Herkert's or because she's mine. I'm mostly hard to love. Another thing we have in common, you and me. *Come close but not too close.* Memories have been my great paramour. How tightly I've held them, fed them like a fast fire. As I would go to gaze at my sleeping children to make sure they were there, so do I go still now to gaze at my memories. To be sure they are whole.

Fresh and sharp and whole, indeed they are, but to what aim? What shall I do with them, all the secrets unbound tonight, the suffocated whispers thrown up to the light?

'I can't make a myth of those mornings, not some quicksilver fiction. What happened can never not belong to me. But after me? Shall I leave it to whine among the stones and trees, resign it to the Fates who, with or without me, called it down? Better, shall I pass it on to Luce? To Filippa? Why? To win their tears, to make them feel the same arrows that pierced me? Were I to do that now at the end, I would become larger to them when I should be growing smaller. They would turn their women's pity on me. If they are to know, I wish it could be *after* me. There is a decency to our growing smaller at the end. A minor-key nocturne, diminishing, *lento, pianissimo*. A blossom folding, consenting to the dusk.

'I suppose they've had their supper by now, Giòrgia and Biagino. If any of the others have returned, Giorgia likely kept them from coming to search for us. Maybe Biagino did,' Antonia tells me as she moves the valises and the other things I'd left packed outside the door, places them near the princess bed. 'Your Byzantine should be wandering in soon. Shall I help you to retake your camp before he does?'

She is unfolding a sheet, flinging it over the mattress, flicking her wrists to get it right, expertly fitting it. I take my place on the other side of the bed. 'That'll do for now,' I tell her, plumping the pillows, the one upon which, a few moments before, she'd rested her head, still damp from her tears.

'Yes. For now, I think it will. Shall we walk?'

I close the lodge door, my hand glancing the sheaf of ginestra fastened under the boar's head, and when I turn around she's looking at me. A hand on her hip, elbow crooked, she looks a tall, embattled, one-winged bird. Featherless, the brown of her dress like pebbly skin, her smile dazed, uncertain of her victory as she is of her defeat. And is she wondering if they are not, after all, the same?

Waves flailing at the rocks below beat the same rhythm as my heart. Face to face, eye to eye, we stand still.

'Resolution?' I ask her.

She waits, still looking at me she waits a long time. A small girl called upon to stand before the class, Antonia knows the answer but can't quite say the words. She places her arms on my shoulders, pulls me closer. Parched, ancient, her voice. She whispers, 'Resolution belongs only to the gods.'

I press my cheek to Antonia's small soft one and she holds it there with her hand.

'Ah, *tesoro mio*—ah, my darling girl, how the Fates would laugh at us, at we scintillas who would suppose ourselves wise enough to gain *resolution*. But they've given us something better, the gods. Something more. They've left us *passion*. The sweetness of that everyday dish of beauty. A bigger dose, a smaller dose, we never know how much they'll dole out but mostly it's enough, I think. Then it's up to us. What we make of it. Our own dose of beauty. *Nothing squandered. The light won't wait, you know.* And so what we do is, well, we climb the hills. Sometimes we climb in a sea-smelling breeze past new green wheat just high enough to quiver. We quiver. Still we stride the road as though we know the way, veer off onto some path or other, ambushing the beasts, pushing deeper into the vastness, bent on the pungent scent of a dream, squinting to read the maps we drew once on the walls of our child hearts. *This is what we do.'*

She slips her arm through mine. The moon spills topaz on the night, makes a yellow fire in the thick green tresses of the oaks, and the faraway chime of Agostino's bells is like the jingling of homeward goats. We are homeward goats, Antonia and me. I think we all are. Climbing the hill once again. Up the hill, back down the hill. As she bends her head down nearer to mine, I incline towards Antonia's shoulder and we are a triangle, one side shorter than the other, making our way up the slope of the white road. *Because this is what we do.*

Without turning to me, Antonia says, 'I've been thinking we should have some small supper. The embers will still be warm in the oven, warm enough to roast a few pieces of bread, and meanwhile I'll wander down among the tomatoes. One is sure to be ripe. First, though, let's sit on the veranda and take small peaceful sips of Viola's fancy red. Would you like that?'

Fine

RECIPES

At first blush, cooking *alla* Toscana seems child's play, calling as it does for relatively simple techniques and nothing of ornaments and flourishes. But beware. When a cuisine is as unadorned, as straightforward as this, it's the perfection of the *materia prima* that becomes sacred. Tuscan authenticity demands perfect elements and this is one of the reasons why it remains a challenge to reproduce beyond its own territories.

Bruschetta con gli asparagi

ROASTED BREAD WITH BRAISED ASPARAGUS

Bruschetta *(bruse-khett'-ah)—the one and only true* bruschetta, *that is—is nothing more nor less than honest country bread toasted lightly on both sides over a wood fire, drizzled generously with that year's good green oil and finished off with a few turns of the sea-salt grinder. The greater world has adopted this ancient way to begin a supper and often not treated it well, topping less than wonderful bread with even less wonderful oil and then laying on all manner of inappropriate bits and pieces. If one chooses to gild the original, it's the innocence of simple roasted vegetables that best exalts it. Baby leeks, spring onions, young garlic are just as good as the asparagus.*

Ingredients

(TO SERVE 4)

- ✥ a wood fire gone to ash or a hot oven broiler
- ✥ fresh green pencil-thin (or thinner) asparagus, washed, dried, stalks trimmed and peeled—about 8–10 per bruschetta
- ✥ extra virgin olive oil

- ½-inch (1.5-cm) trenchers of good country bread
- sea salt

Place the asparagus on a grate directly over the ashes and roast, turning them often, basting with the olive oil until charred and tender; remove to a plate. If roasting under a broiler, place the asparagus on an oven sheet and roast in the same manner. The process will want a few extra minutes if roasting in the oven.

When the asparagus are nearly done, begin toasting the bread. Ideally, the two elements should be ready at about the same time. Drizzle the hot bread with oil, lay over the asparagus, drizzle on more oil. A few turns of the salt grinder and they're ready to serve.

Caterina's carabaccia

A SOUP OF CINNAMON-SCENTED ONIONS AND PEAS IN THE MANNER OF CATERINA DE MEDICI

It seems that Caterina, wife of Henry II of France, adored spring peas, and tales of her overindulgence—in peas, in other

passions—are legion. A holdover from the medieval gastronomic canons, it's the unexpected whiff of cinnamon which characterises the soup, transforms it from a homey dish to a rarefied one. There seems no question that this formula was the precursor to what has become France's soupe à l'oignon gratinée.

Ingredients

- 4 tbsp extra virgin olive oil
- 1 tbsp unsalted butter
- 4 large yellow onions, peeled and thinly sliced
- 1 tbsp sugar
- 2 tsp ground cinnamon
- sea salt and freshly cracked white pepper
- 3 cups good beef broth, preferably homemade
- 1 cup dry white wine
- 500 g fresh English peas, shelled and poached in water for 5–7 minutes, drained (the pot liquor reserved) and puréed (tiny peas, frozen and prepped in the same manner, may be substituted, though to a lesser result)

- ✧ 1 cup just-grated Parmigiano
- ✧ 6 ½-inch (1.5-cm) slices coarse-textured bread, lightly toasted and rubbed with extra virgin olive oil

Warm the olive oil and melt the butter in a large soup pot. Add the onions, sautéing them to translucence; sprinkle the onions with the sugar and cinnamon, stirring to coat them well, add the salt and white pepper and cook the onions over a very low flame, stirring them often, caramelising them in the sugar, colouring, scenting them with the cinnamon, until they collapse into a soft jam—about an hour. This process yields the delicate base on which the soup is built. Add the broth, wine, the purée of peas and the reserved cooking liquor, bringing the mass to the simmer and cooking the soup over a low flame for 10 minutes. Off the heat, add the Parmigiano, stirring it well. Ladle the soup, hot or tepid, over the olive oil toast in warmed, deep soup plates, threading the whole with a few drops more of oil.

Fagioli al fiasco sotto le cenere

White beans braised in a flask under cinders

Tuscans are known throughout other regions of the peninsula as mangiafagioli, *bean-eaters, and the repertoire of traditional soups and stews almost always stars a creamy white bean. The varieties include but are hardly limited to: cannelloni, corona, purgatorio, soranini, toscanello and even the giant, flat bean called coco which is of French origin. White beans cooked slowly either in a bottle buried in the ashes of a wood fire or in a terracotta pot in a lazy oven result in an extraordinary, almost mousse-like creaminess.*

Ingredients
(to serve 6)

- ↭ 350 g dried white beans (see list above), soaked overnight, drained, pre-cooked in boiling, salted water for an hour and drained again
- ↭ 2 cups water
- ↭ ½ cup extra virgin olive oil
- ↭ a branch of rosemary
- ↭ 3 cloves of garlic, peeled and crushed

- 6–8 leaves of fresh sage
- sea salt and freshly cracked pepper
- additional extra virgin olive oil, to taste
- ½ cup finely chopped, peeled, pipped tomatoes (optional)
- crusty bread, to serve

Place the beans in a wine bottle (preferably a bulbous-bottomed chianti bottle); add the water, oil, rosemary, garlic and sage; fashion a stopper for the bottle with a piece of cloth, leaving room for building steam to exit and hence not explode the bottle. Bury the bottle in the white ashes of a hearth and go to bed. Upon awakening, the house will be perfumed and (the beans having absorbed the oil) the water vaporised. Remove the stopper and pour the beans into a bowl, salting and peppering them generously, removing the rosemary and garlic, and adding, perhaps, a few more drops of oil.

To cook them on top of the stove, mix all the elements in a heavy pot and braise them, the pot lid barely askew, for 2 hours or so over a quiet flame so the liquids barely move. Alternatively, bring the mass to a simmer on top of the stove in a terracotta vessel with a lid or a soup pot with a lid and place the pot, tightly covered, in a 300°F (150°C) oven for 2 hours. The addition of half a cup of finely chopped, peeled, pipped tomatoes causes no harm. Serve the beans warm, at room temperature or even cool, with a few drops more of oil, great hunks of crusty bread and a good honest red.

Arista

ROASTED LOIN OF PORK IN THE MANNER OF THE FLORENTINES

The word arista *is not, as many propose, the dialect version of* arrosto *or 'roast'. The oldest of tomes insist that the name for Tuscany's celebrated spit-roasted loin of pork sprung from a glorious compliment paid by visiting Greek noblemen at the Florentine court. Having been served several preparatory dishes cooked in harmony with the Savonarola's sumptuary laws (the monk dictated the number of dishes, their elements and the mode in which they might be prepared and presented, exclusive of any 'lavishness and ostentation'), a simple roasted meat was presented to the Greek guests. Whether an expression of relief from the austerity of the* earlier courses or simply a tribute to the scent of its garlic- and rosemary-perfumed flesh, it is written that: 'those dour-robed Greeks feasted upon it voraciously, neither speaking to nor listening to the discourse around them. And when it was finished, they rose to their feet in a chorus of "Arista! Arista!"' Thus arista, the root of the word aristocrat and intending 'powerful because best', was henceforth embraced by the Florentines. Here is an oven-braised reading every bit as 'aristocratic'. It differs only minimally from the version mentioned in the narrative.

Ingredients

(TO SERVE 10)

- a 3.5-kg loin of pork with its rib bones, the flesh cut almost fully but not quite so from the bones, the bones cracked for easier carving; all of this accomplished by a sympathetic butcher
- a large head of purple garlic, its cloves peeled and crushed
- ⅔ cup fresh rosemary leaves
- ½ cup extra virgin olive oil
- sea salt and freshly cracked pepper

- ❧ a branch or several thick sprigs of wild rosemary
- ❧ a bottle of *vernaccia* or other crisp, acidic white wine

Cut 2.5-cm incisions over all the surfaces of the pork. In the workbowl of a food processor fitted with a steel blade, or in a large mortar, process or pound the garlic, rosemary leaves and oil to a rough paste. Add generous amounts of salt and pepper and combine the elements well. Massage the paste deeply into the incisions and over the entire surface of the flesh. Secure the flesh to the bones with butcher's twine and permit the pork to drink in the flavours of the paste for several hours, covered and in a cool place or overnight in the refrigerator. Place it in a heavy roasting pan not much larger than its own bulk and roast it at 480°F (250°C), turning it every 10 minutes or so. Each time you turn the roast, use the wild rosemary branch or several sprigs of rosemary tied together as a brush to baste the pork with its own juices. Keep turning and basting at 10-minute intervals until all sides are deeply golden.

Remove the roasting pan from the oven and slowly add the wine to a depth of 5 cm. Reserve the remaining

wine. Cover the pan and return it to the hot oven. Ten
minutes later, lower the heat to 350°F (180°C) and braise
the pork, covered, for an additional 1½ hours or until
the flesh is beginning to fall from its bones. Carefully
remove the pork to a deep plate, cover loosely with foil
and give it a 15-minute rest while proceeding with the
sauce. Place the roasting pan over a lively flame and
add the remaining wine (yes, the rest of the bottle),
reducing the pan juices by one-third. Snip the strings
on the pork and carve it, somewhat thickly, between
its bones. Serve with its sauce. A purée of white beans
or broad beans flavoured with fennel seed is a worthy
accompaniment.

Schiacciata con l'uve del vino

FLATBREAD WITH WINE GRAPES

A legacy of the Etruscans and their harvest celebrations, this is
perhaps the most ancient bread still surviving in the present-day
repertoire. Sending up a maddening perfume as it bakes, the

taste—sweet, peppery, spicy, the bread itself still crunchy though
wet with the juice of bursting grapes—is like no other.

Ingredients

(TO SERVE 6–8)

- 1½ cups all-purpose flour
- 1 tbsp light brown sugar
- 2 packages active dry yeast or 2 small cubes of fresh yeast
- 1 cup warm water
- ½ cup extra virgin olive oil
- 3 tbsp fresh rosemary leaves, minced
- 2 tbsp fennel seeds, crushed
- 2 tbsp anise seeds, crushed
- 1 tbsp freshly cracked pepper
- 4 cups all-purpose flour, extra
- 1 tbsp sea salt
- ¼ cup light brown sugar, extra
- 2 eggs
- green, purple and red grapes trimmed into small bunches of about 6–8 grapes each—about 12 bunches in all

- ⅔ cup granulated sugar
- ground black pepper

In a large workbowl, combine 1½ cups flour, 1 tablespoon sugar, yeast and water, allowing the mass to activate for 15 minutes; meanwhile, in a small pan, warm the oil and add the rosemary, fennel, anise and pepper, permitting the spices to perfume the oil for 10 minutes over a quiet flame. Remove from the flame and set aside.

Return to the workbowl and add the additional 4 cups of flour, the salt, ¼ cup of light brown sugar, the eggs and all but 2 tablespoons of the spiced oil with its seeds, incorporating the elements well. Turn the mass out onto a lightly floured board and knead for 5 minutes. Place the dough in a lightly oiled bowl and permit the mass to rise for 30 minutes. Deflate the dough and roll it or flatten it with your hands into a rather free-form circle or rectangle and position it on a parchment-lined sheet. Press the small bunches of grapes into the dough, drizzle them with the remaining 2 tablespoons of the spiced oil—seeds and all—dust them liberally with the granulated sugar and grind over generous amounts of pepper. Cover the bread with a clean kitchen towel and leave it to rise for 40 minutes. Bake the *schiacciata* at 400°F (200°C) for 25–30 minutes or until it is golden and swollen, the grapeskins bursting. Cool the bread on a rack for 5 minutes.

Serve it very warm, warm, or tepid, by itself with a *novello* (a term for the Italian version of Beaujolais—a just-vintered, unaged, low-alcohol red full of fresh fruit flavours). A more unusual idea: serve it as a supper bread to accompany a rich braise of beef or pork or alongside grilled meats.

Le tortucce della contadina

FRIED ROSEMARY-SCENTED FLATBREAD IN THE MANNER OF THE FARMER'S WIFE

These luscious breads may be the ultimate and universal crowd pleasers. It is highly recommended that the cook not make these breads all alone in the kitchen and then carry them forth as magic provender. The very process of stretching the dough, heaving it into the bubbling oil, watching the breads puff and turn golden, lifting

*them out and onto paper-lined plates to drain, whispering sea salt
over them is all part of their enjoyment, moments to share with
those who will eat them. Invite guests into the kitchen, open a few
well-cooled bottles of vernaccia, pour, raise your glasses and begin.
Here we eat tortucce with slices of mortadella or prosciutto crudo
nostrano (the local artisanal prosciutto). A hard act to follow, these
tortucce, so that only a rustic soup or pasta seems appropriate to
complete the supper.*

Ingredients

(TO SERVE 8)

- 1 cake of fresh yeast (18 g)
- 1 cup tepid water
- 2 tbsp extra virgin olive oil
- ½ cup whole milk
- 2 tbsp unsalted butter, softened
- 2 cups unbleached all-purpose flour
- 1 generous tsp fine sea salt
- 3 tbsp rosemary leaves, chopped very finely
- a large heavy deep skillet or deep fryer
- oil for deep-frying (in Orvieto we have good
  oil in such abundance that we sometimes

use it to deep-fry these breads; alternatively,
substitute peanut oil)

Crumble the yeast into the bottom of a large, slightly warmed bowl; pour in ½ cup of the water and stir (veteran breadbakers use the swirling motion of one hand for this); let the mixture stand for a few minutes then agitate it again. Stir in the remaining water, the oil, milk, butter, flour, salt and rosemary to form a loose mass. Turn the mass out onto a lightly floured board or marble and knead until satiny, about 10 minutes.

Wash and dry the mixing bowl and, while it's still warm, pour in a few drops of olive oil; add the dough and turn it over and over in the oil until it's coated nicely. Cover the bowl tightly with plastic wrap. (Many country cooks place a folded tablecloth or even a smallish blanket over the rising bowl. Though this has no scientific purpose it somehow satisfies the maternal pull which bread-baking inspires.) Allow the dough to rise until doubled in size, about 2 hours depending upon the weather and the temperature in the kitchen.

When the dough has properly risen, deflate it with two or three hefty punches and set the frying vessel with the oil over a medium flame (heating the oil over a high flame will leave cool patches and cause uneven cooking). While the oil is heating, begin pinching off about 50 grams of dough and stretching it into thin rounds; some cooks roll the dough with a pin, many more thin it into shape with the tips of the fingers. Though this latter method takes a bit of practice, it offers much more fun than the pin. Here's where guests can be helpful. When the oil is hot but not smoking, slip in the first batch of *tortucce*. They will immediately puff and bubble, and begin bobbing about in the oil. Let them be for 2 minutes before beginning to turn them over. When they are deeply golden, remove with a wire skimmer to a paper-towel-lined baking sheet or tray. A grinding of salt. These won't wait. The cool wine, the hot *tortucce* . . .

Castagnaccio

CHESTNUT FLOUR PUDDING

Because the period in which the narrative is set was spring and summer, castagnaccio *was not part of Antonia's menus. But each*

*and every time I subsequently visited Castelletto in the autumn, it
was always served. In fact, every Tuscan I've ever known who is
(or was) past the flower of his youth always gets around to stirring
up this traditional autumn pudding. He always gets around, too,
to telling stories—often sad ones—of childhood* castagnaccio.

Along with polenta, castagnaccio *was the historical survival
food of the peasants during wars and other brutal acts of man and
the gods. Even the suffix of the word—*accio—*denotes something
less than refined, perhaps less than desirable. Yet with the suffusing
effects of time, the days of misery have taken on a kind of nostalgia
so that there is hardly a rural family who does not eagerly await
the late October arrival of chestnut flour in the local markets.
The half-kilo cloth sacks tied with kitchen string are carried
home, the fine, satiny chestnut flour sprinkled,* alla pioggia—*like
rain—into cold water and stirred with a wooden spoon until the
batter is smooth. Plumped raisins, minced rosemary, a fistful of
pine nuts, a spoonful of oil, a sprinkling of salt are added (though
these were imponderable luxuries in meaner times) and the batter
is poured into a round tin—the most battered and well used in
the house—and baked in a lively oven until the pudding has set,
its surface cracked and a bit dry.*

*Serve the pudding warm or at room temperature with a glass
of red or a tinier one of* vin santo. *The locals tend to serve it*

*warm, enriched with a dollop of that morning's ewe's-milk ricotta
as foil for the pudding's unusual smoky flavour. They enrich it,
too, always with a story.*

Ingredients

(TO SERVE 6)

500 g chestnut flour (available in fancy markets
    and Italian neighbourhood groceries; check
    the date as chestnut flour has a shelf life of
    no more than 6 months)

cold water

½ cup pine nuts, lightly roasted

½ cup raisins plumped in warm water and
    drained

2 tsp rosemary leaves, minced

1 tbsp olive oil

½ tsp sea salt

Place the flour in a medium bowl and pour in water in a
thin stream, stirring all the while with a wooden spoon,
until the mass is the consistency of a thin batter. The
amount of water varies immensely depending on the

texture of the chestnut flour—about 2½ cups or more. Add the pine nuts, the raisins, the rosemary, the olive oil and salt, beating the elements well. Pour the batter into an oiled mould and bake it at 450°F (230°C) for 30 minutes or until it obtains the dark look of a crackled chocolate cake. Serve warm or at room temperature.

Ricotta di pecora al miele di castagne pepato

EWE'S-MILK RICOTTA WITH CHESTNUT HONEY AND FRESHLY CRACKED PEPPER

Not a sweet and not a savoury, this is what is known as a fine pasto *(as opposed to an* antipasto, *which is served before the meal, this is served to end the meal; many still believe, in error, that* antipasto *signifies 'before the pasta', but the word is* pasto, *meal). In any case, it was this sort of dish, composed of elements foraged or at hand, which once sustained shepherds and country folk. Though this was served in a delicate and refined way that first evening I dined at Castelletto, I have also been served it at the edge of a sheepfold in the meadows of Buon Respiro above*

Orvieto: ewe's-milk curds straight from a cooking pot hung over an oakwood fire, dolloped into a wooden bowl and stuck with a long dripping shard of honeycomb. With no pepper grinder at hand out there under the stars, my friend Orfeo pulled a few hazelnuts from his foraging sack, pounded them open with a stone and, with his pocket knife, chipped them over the curds. Somehow these two memories of essentially the same dish distil what I like best about living in Italy: the universal levelling influence which food creates across the strata of society.

ACKNOWLEDGEMENTS

Fernando Filiberto-Maria

amore mio

With love and appreciation for the nearness of:

Erich Brandon Knox

Annette Barlow

Giuseppina Sugaro Pettinelli

Mary Jo Martin

Rosalie Siegel

Sylvia and Harold Epstein

Stefania Rolfi and Marco Pepe
Ilaria Moscatelli and Gianluca Pepe
Francesca Pierangeli and Leonardo Napoli.

A special wish for the sweetest little girl in Orvieto, Lavinia Petrangeli, and her beautiful family.

It was my editor, Catherine Milne, who with a rare sensitivity and passion, took me by the hand, her other hand slashing a path through the woods where she found me.

It was Clara Finlay, superb editor's editor, who polished the text with an extraordinary *raffinatezza* and who helped me to remember that to understand and to be understood causes the most durable happiness of all.

In loving memory
Daniela Caiello Picaria and Giancarlo Bianchini da Todi